CLASSROOM AND SMALL GROUP ACTIVITIES

FOR TEACHERS, COUNSELORS, AND OTHER HELPING PROFESSIONALS

VOL. II

Pre-K–12 & Beyond

Other Awareness

Self-Control

Group Cooperation

Tommie R. Radd, PhD

© 2003 by Grow With Guidance®
10808 Larimore Avenue
Omaha, Nebraska 68164
800/377-1514   Fax 402/496-0925
gwg@allsucceed.com
www.allsucceed.com

ISBN #1-878317-46-6

All rights reserved. No part of the material protected by this copyright notice may be reproduced or used in any form or by any means electronic or mechanical, including photocopying, recording or by any information storage and retrieval system without prior written permission of the copyright owner.

NOTICE: Grow With Guidance® grants permission to the user of this material to copy the forms for teaching purposes. Duplication of this material for commercial use is prohibited.

- Contents -

PREFACE	ix
INTRODUCTION	1
OTHER AWARENESS	5-162
SECTION DEFINITIONS	6
Manners in Action	7
Information Sharing	8
Other Perspectives	9
Permission to Search	10
Friendship Factors	11
Needs in Lyrics	12
Seeing the Positive in Others	13
Suggestions or Demands?	14
Handling Frustrations	15
Positive Expectations	16
A Buddy to Help Others	17
Positive Introductions	18
Which Side Is Best?	19
Sending Messages	20
Effective Listening	21
Relating to Others	22
Relating To Others Activity Sheet	23
Responsibility for Others' Experiences	24
What Do You Wish?	25
Election Experience	26
Helping Experiences	27
Learning About Sharing	28
Learning About Sharing Activity Sheet	29
Positive Feedback	30
Leadership	31
People Information	32
People Information Activity Sheet	33
Mystery Friend	34
Student Sing-a-long	35
The Helpful Way to Say It Game	36
Acknowledging Others	37
Interdependence	38
Understanding Need Blocks	39
Super Sportsmanship	40
Understanding Interpretation Differences	41

- Contents -

OTHER AWARENESS (CONTINUED)

The Rights of Others	42
The Rights of Others Activity Sheet	43
Buddy Business	44
What Are My Rights?	45
Responsibilities	46
Feeling Situations	47
Handling Different Opinions	48
Emotional Maturity	49
Problem Box Support	50
Security With Others	51
Spread the Joy	52
Developing Positive Human Relations	53
Applying the Definition of Average	54
Identify the Mystery Person	55
Expressions About Others	56
The Impact of Smiling	57
Understanding Your Needs	58
The Impact of the Bill of Rights	59
Prejudice or Fact?	60
Prejudice or Fact? Activity Sheet	61
Bullying Role-Play	62
Giving and Receiving Respect	63
Promoting Understanding	64
Group Interests	65
I'm a Computer	66
Describing Others	67
Who Are You? Game	68
Behavior Surprise	69
Magic Gift	70
A Positive Focus	71
The Power of Humor	72
Group Information Search	73
Group Uniqueness	74
Using Our Imaginations	75
Special Identity Experience	76
Gather All the Facts	77
Individual Differences	78

- Contents -

OTHER AWARENESS (CONTINUED)

The Joy of Sharing	79
Complement Experience	80
Growth Rate Differences	81
Magic Wand	82
The Impact of Our Needs	83
Alike or Different?	84
Your Point of View?	85
Your Original Print	86
Your Original Print Activity Sheet	87
Interview Experience	88
Interview Experience Activity Sheet	89
All Viewpoints	90
Basic Similarities	91
Animal Instruction	92
Your Talents and Abilities	93
Ways We Differ	94
Who Is It? Game	95
Identification Game	96
Phrases That Describe	97
Decision Puzzle	98
Decision Puzzle Clues	99
What Is Happiness?	100
What Is Happiness? Activity Sheet	101
Student for the Day	102
Traits of Being Friendly	103
Handling Winning Desires	104
Anger and Behavior	105
Charades	106
Charades Activity Sheet	107
Posture Expression	108
Impact of Environment	109
Talking Differences	110
Talking Differences Activity Sheet	111
Attitude Factors	112
Differences of Opinion	113
What's the Feeling?	114
Gesture Demonstrations	115

© 2003
www.allsucceed.com

- Contents -

OTHER AWARENESS (CONTINUED)

Sharing Fun	116
Enjoyment of Sharing	117
Story Feelings Faces	118
Feelings Role-Play	119
Cartoon Creation	120
Colors and Feelings	121
Empathy for Others	122
Helping Others	123
Honesty Experience	124
Handling Anger	125
Teacher Communication	126
Expressing Fears	127
Handling Classroom Anger	128
Building Bridges	129
Define Hurtful Behavior	130
Sharing Experiences	131
Different Reactions	132
Different Reactions Activity Sheet	133
Owner Location Game	134
Posture Communication	135
A Radiant Glow	136
The Impact of Aggression	137
Ways Teachers Help	138
Concerns Survey	139
The Impact of Feelings	140
Including Others	141
Need for Safety	142
Need for Safety Activity Sheet	143
Communicating Gestures	144
Communicating Gestures Activity Sheet	145
Exploring Gestures	146
Role-Play a Hurtful Action	147
Helpful and Hurtful Actions	148
Feeling Situations	149
Hurtful Actions in Fairy Tales	150
Guess the Feeling	151
Feeling Word Communication	152
Expanding Feeling Vocabulary	153

- Contents -

OTHER AWARENESS (CONTINUED)
Being New	154
Being New Activity Sheet	155
Hurtful Behaviors	156
Guess Their Answers	157
Assertion and Aggression Projects	158
Problem Experiences	159
Feeling Comparisons Game	160
Feeling Comparisons Game Activity Sheet	161

SELF-CONTROL   **163-236**
SECTION DEFINITIONS   **164**
What Would You Do?	165
Seeing My Future	166
Seeing My Future Activity Sheet	167
Developing Self-Discipline	168
Personal Reflection	169
Giving Complements	170
Becoming Secure	171
Ways Others See You	172
Ways Others See You Activity Sheet	173
Becoming What You Wish	174
Influence of Experiences	175
Feelings and Self-Control	176
Feelings and Self-Control Activity Sheet	177
Characteristics for Student Success	178
Characteristics for Student Success Activity Sheet	179
Attitude Survey	180
Attitude Survey Activity Sheet	181
Working At Home	182
Becoming a Leader	183
Needs Awareness	184
Needs Awareness Activity Sheet	185
Meeting Your Needs	186
Meeting Your Needs Activity Sheet	187
Meeting Basic Needs Through Leisure	188
Meeting Basic Needs Through Leisure Activity Sheet	189
Assessing Your Interests	190
Assessing Your Interests Activity Sheet	191

- Contents -

SELF-CONTROL (CONTINUED)

Hurtful Behaviors	192
When to Ask for Help	193
Dreams of the Future	194
Communicating Progress	195
Describe Yourself	196
Special Job Role-Play	197
Handling Restlessness	198
Mirror Person	199
Assessing Change	200
Assessing Change Activity Sheet	201
Evaluating Your Work	202
Home Responsibilities	203
What's Your Guess?	204
Control Your Emotions	205
Ways Others Influence Behavior	206
The Impact of Rules	207
Handling Anxieties	208
Ways to Verbalize Anger	209
Controlling Your Activity	210
Thinking Chair	211
Handling Peer Pressure	212
Handling Peer Pressure Role-Play	213
Behavior Problems and Solutions	214
Choices and Consequences	215
Create a Story	216
No Conflict Allowed	217
What Would Happen?	218
Feelings in New Situations	219
If That Doesn't Work . . .	220
Owning Your Behavior	221
Telling or Tattling?	222
Appropriate Behavior	223
Talk It Over	224
Challenge Bank	225
Group Pattern Experience	226
Handle Your Anger	227

© 2003
www.allsucceed.com

- Contents -

SELF-CONTROL (CONTINUED)
Anger Discussions	228
Anger Discussions Activity Sheet	229
Sentence Completion	230
Sentence Completion Activity Sheet	231
Televise Solutions	232
The Impact of Needs on Actions	233
Create Learning Stories	234
Assertive Behavior	235
Controlling Aggression	236

GROUP COOPERATION   **237-290**
SECTION DEFINITIONS   **238**
Conformity Experience	239
Your Family Map	240
Where Are You?	241
Group Work Experience	242
How Do You Work?	243
Creating New Countries	244
Get The Whole Picture	245
Everyone Benefits	246
Things Done Well	247
Sharing Traditions	248
Becoming Independent	249
Every-Day Routines	250
Positive Home Environment	251
Learning From Animals	252
Jealousy Awareness	253
Improving Relationships	254
Considering Family Members	255
Strength in Numbers	256
Group Identity	257
Mosaic Experience	258
An Effective Follower	259
Sharing a List	260
Creating Family Harmony	261
Follow My Lead	262
Follow My Lead Activity Sheet	263
Cooperation Experiences	264

- Contents -

GROUP COOPERATION (CONTINUED)

Career Cooperation	265
Classroom Improvement	266
Improving Communication	267
Improving Cooperation	268
Using Our Senses	269
Who Said It?	270
Going on the Air	271
Group Clean-Up Day	272
Sharing Mirror	273
Balance Experiences	274
Effective Leadership	275
Group Problem Solving	276
Learning Cooperation	277
Sweet Rewards	278
Password Game	279
Rope-Jumping Experience	280
Responsibility in Groups	281
Family Challenges	282
Sharing Collage	283
Create a Mural	284
Responsibilities and Rules	285
Student Government	286
Group Participation Experience	287
My House and Family	288
Assertive Group Effects	289

FEELING WORDS LISTS AND CARDS   **291-306**

Feeling Words Lists	293-295
Feeling Words Cards	296-305
Creative Corners	306-307

PREFACE

Dear Professional,

I'm excited to offer you *Classroom and Small Group Activities for Teachers, Counselors, and Other Helping Professionals: Volumes I and II.* These books are designed to provide valuable, supplemental materials that can really make a difference in the quality of your programs. I welcome your questions and feedback. You may contact me at gwg@allsucceed.com or on the Web at www.allsucceed.com. Please let me know if I can be of assistance. My goal is to support your success.

Best wishes,

Tommie R. Radd, PhD

INTRODUCTION

Classroom and Small Group Activities for Teachers, Counselors, and Other Helping Professionals: Volume II is a book of classroom and small group activities for pre-K–12 and beyond. Volume II includes over 250 activities and activity sheets (where appropriate) in the strand areas of Other Awareness, Self-Control, and Group Cooperation. Volume I includes over 250 activities and activity sheets (where appropriate) in the strand areas of Self and Decision Making/Problem Solving. Both volumes are designed for use in areas of the school educational and counseling programs and may be supplements for *The Grow With Guidance® System* or your comprehensive, developmental guidance and counseling program. The special features of this book are described in the following sections.

Flexibility and Use in Different Program Settings

- **Classroom Group Guidance:** The activities are ideal for classroom use as a supplement for your pre-k–12, developmental classroom group guidance portion of the program. *Classroom and Small Group Activities for Teachers, Counselors, and Other Helping Professionals: Volumes I and II* are in the same strand areas as *The Grow With Guidance® System* activities. They do not include the goals, competencies, results, and evaluation plan that the System activities include. *The Grow With Guidance® System* and *Classroom and Small Group Activities for Teachers, Counselors, and Other Helping Professionals: Volumes I and II* strand areas are congruent with the guidance and counseling program requirements of most state and national models.

- **Groups:** The activities are ideal for all types of small and large group programs, including small group counseling.

- **Individuals:** Some activities are appropriate for use in individual counseling sessions or for individual follow-up after classroom group guidance, small group counseling, and other types of small and large group experiences.

- **Family and Other Adult Groups:** Many activities are appropriate for use with various parent and other adult groups.

Special Topics and Group Programs

Volumes I and II can be incorporated into programs and groups for all of these special topics: Academic Achievement, School-to-Career, Drug-free Schools, Safe Schools, Character Education, Social Skills, Invitational Education, Bullying and Harassment, Peace Education, Cooperation, Special Needs Students, and many others.

Pre-K–12, and Beyond

Classroom and Small Group Activities for Teachers, Counselors, and Other Helping Professionals: Volumes I and II include activities that can be used with, and would appeal to, a broad range of age groups.

Over 250 Activities in Each Volume

There are over 250 activity choices each for Volumes I and II. The wide range of quality activity options is a great value.

Easy-To-Use Book Format

Classroom and Small Group Activities for Teachers, Counselors, and Other Helping Professionals: Volumes I and II have an easy-to-use design that allows you to duplicate activities and activity sheets easily and quickly. The table of contents clearly lists activities by strand so that you can find them easily.

Easy-To-Use Activity Format

Each activity page includes the activity strand area (e.g., Other Awareness), a statement of Purpose, Materials needed, and clear directions for easy use. Activity sheets are located next to the corresponding activity page.

Special Feeling Words Lists and Cards Section

Classroom and Small Group Activities for Teachers, Counselors, and Other Helping Professionals: Volumes I and II include a special Feeling Words Lists and Cards section that are used with specific activities. These pages can also be used as an option or as a resource for other activities. In many cases, the words may be used as both feeling and descriptive words. A general feeling words cards page is included at the back of the book so that students can write additional feeling and descriptive words.

Unique Creative Corner Feature

It is important to develop student creativity and higher-ordered thinking. Many activity sheets include a Creative Corner section that students can use to develop creative expression of the activity purpose (students are asked to draw or express themselves in these sections of the activity sheet). General Creative Corner activity pages are included at the back of the book for use with any activity where additional student support and follow-up is desired.

Cooperative Approach and Focus

Classroom and Small Group Activities for Teachers, Counselors, and Other Helping Professionals: Volumes I and II were created to support cooperation. All activities provide opportunities for students to cooperate with each other. There is a clear expectation for students to acknowledge and treat themselves and others with a respectful and cooperative spirit. Most activities can be implemented easily in a cooperative learning process and structure. The activity games are student-friendly; most games include an option for the activity to be organized based on a cooperative model.

Service Learning

Several activities include service learning projects as possible applications of the activity concepts. These activities provide additional opportunities for students to apply activity skills and to bring their activity experiences to life situations.

Integration of Technology

Many activities can be integrated with electronic learning initiatives and numerous technical applications (specific instructions for the integration of technology are not included due to the different resources and to the fast moving nature of technology). The activities that include newspapers, magazines, pictures, video tape and audio tape recorders, art supplies, drawings, and reference information materials can easily accommodate technology integration.

OTHER AWARENESS

Other Awareness:

An awareness of the needs of others; a willingness to acknowledge them and to function accordingly.

An awareness of the uniqueness and differences of people.

The ability to define and describe feelings related to personal experiences.

- Other Awareness -

MANNERS IN ACTION

Purpose: Help students to learn and acknowledge the needs of others and to behave accordingly.

Tell the students:

> It is important that we are aware of the needs of others. This activity helps us learn more about their needs. Please listen, follow directions, and participate.

Discuss with the class the importance of manners and how they help one to succeed both at home and at school.

Discuss with the group the meaning of the Golden Rule.

Ask the students to brainstorm and list on the board rules of courtesy for the class to follow at home and at school, such as:

1. Let others talk without interrupting.

2. Excuse yourself if you walk between two people.

3. Say, "Please" and "Thank you."

Role-play each of the manner suggestions and determine the best times to use that manner. After each role-play, ask the students to share ways that behavior may help them get along better with others. Discuss their feelings about the behavior.

Ask students to have a "Manners Check-Up" to determine how they are doing. Encourage family input as appropriate.

Notes:

Materials:
None

Notes:

- Other Awareness -

INFORMATION SHARING

Purpose: Help students learn the uniqueness and differences of people.

Tell the students:

> It is important that we are aware of the uniqueness and differences of others so that we may feel happier and get along better. This activity helps us learn more about others. Please listen, follow directions, and participate.

Have the students tell the group how the following people do things to help others:

doctor	parent
teacher	police officer
truck driver	nurse
secretary	firefighter
student	librarian

Ask students to find additional information about each and share the information with the group. Ask students to determine the characteristics that help the persons do their jobs.

Select additional people to add to the list as appropriate for the group.

Materials:

Resource information

Notes:

- Other Awareness -

OTHER PERSPECTIVES

Purpose: Help students learn the uniqueness and differences of people.

Tell the students:

> It is important that we are aware of the uniqueness and differences of others so that we may feel happier and get along better. This activity helps us learn more about others. Please listen, follow directions, and participate.

Divide the group into three smaller groups, naming one "elves," another "giants," and the last "norms." Tell the elves to imagine that they are no bigger than their thumbs and ask the giants to imagine that they are tall enough to reach a cloud. The norms remain just as they are.

Give copies of three cards to each group. One card would read, "Describe a big garden of flowers." Another would read, "Describe a cow." And the third card would read, "Describe a tree."

After allowing time for discussion, call on a spokesman for each group to describe the first card, then proceed to cards 2 and 3.

The accuracy of each group's perspective is not as important as the effort put into "seeing" the object in terms of its size. (Have students switch groups to give all the opportunity to be in each group.)

Discuss viewpoints and perspectives. Expand with more empathic-evoking challenges (i.e., describe most likeable, most quiet, etc.).

Materials:

Three sets of three directions cards

Notes:

- Other Awareness -

PERMISSION TO SEARCH

Purpose: Help students to learn and acknowledge the needs of others and to behave accordingly.

Tell the students:

> It is important that we are aware of the needs of others. This activity helps us learn more about their needs. Please listen, follow directions, and participate.

Select a student judge who will issue search warrants.

Ask half of the students to leave the room.

The other half of the group hides an object in one of the desks in the room. The rest of the group comes in and asks for clues to the hiding place. Such clues as "It's in one of the desks by the windows" might be given.

If a student thinks he knows the hiding place, he asks the judge for a warrant that gives permission to look in one of the desks.

He describes his reasons for thinking the object is in a certain desk, and the judge decides whether he receives a warrant. This continues until the object is found by a student, who then becomes judge.

After the game has been played, describe a case that was thrown out of court because evidence was collected without a warrant. Was dismissal of the case fair? Did it protect anyone's rights?

This might lead to a discussion on the rights of everyone involved in search warrants and search and seizure.

Materials:
None

- Other Awareness -

FRIENDSHIP FACTORS

Purpose: Help students learn to define and describe feelings related to personal experiences with others.

Tell the students:

> It is important that we know the way we feel about others and understand ways of explaining those feelings. This activity helps us learn more about the needs of others. Please listen, follow directions, and participate.

"Best friend" is a phrase commonly heard by people of all ages. Ask the students to discuss the advantages and disadvantages of having a best friend.

Explore in depth the idea of possessiveness; that is, some people feel that their best friends are theirs and theirs alone. They are extremely possessive and jealous if others want to be friends with "their" friend.

Point out the unfairness of this attitude and discuss reasons that someone may choose to feel this way.

Suggested questioning:

1. What is a best friend?

2. Describe your best friend, including positive qualities.

3. How are you a best friend?

4. Explain ways of having more than one friend at a time.

5. Explain the benefits of having many friends.

Notes:

Materials:
None

Notes:

- Other Awareness -

NEEDS IN LYRICS

Purpose: Help students to learn and acknowledge the needs of others and to behave accordingly.

Tell the students:

> It is important that we are aware of the needs of others. This activity helps us learn more about their needs. Please listen, follow directions, and participate.

The lyrics of current songs often concentrate on people, their needs, and how their needs are satisfied. Ask the group to suggest songs of this type and to bring in songs to hear. Ask the students to listen to and discuss these songs by asking the following questions:

1. What behavior is being expressed in the song?

2. What needs are expressed in the lyrics?

3. How do the lyrics suggest meeting the needs?

4. How does the individual's behavior affect others?

5. How does the individual's behavior affect him or herself?

6. What may have motivated the composer to write the song?

Provide copies of song lyrics for each student as the song is played.

Materials:

Songs and lyrics

- Other Awareness -

SEEING THE POSITIVE IN OTHERS

Purpose: Help students learn the uniqueness and differences of people.

Tell the students:

It is important that we are aware of uniqueness and differences of others so that we may feel happier and get along better. This activity helps us learn more about others. Please listen, follow directions, and participate.

Discuss with the class the importance of seeing positive qualities in other people as well as in themselves.

Ask for volunteers who are able to see positive qualities in other people and who are willing to talk about these qualities.

The first student begins by saying, "I am thinking about someone in this room. One positive quality about this person is _____."

The student continues naming positive qualities until someone identifies the mystery person.

The student who guesses correctly has the next turn.

Notes:

Materials:

None

13

Notes:

- Other Awareness -

SUGGESTIONS OR DEMANDS?

Purpose: Help students to learn and acknowledge the needs of others and to behave accordingly.

Tell the students:

> It is important that we are aware of the needs of others. This activity helps us learn more about their needs. Please listen, follow directions, and participate.

This game helps students see the difference between a reaction to a suggestion and a reaction to a demand. Tell the students something that one student said in an undiplomatic way.

For example, two students wanted some milk. One student said, "Gimme some milk!" The other student said, "_____."
(Ask someone to suggest a diplomatic way to say the same thing.)

Continue with other situation examples and statements.

Ask students to determine ways of applying activity ideas in other life situations and determine the effects of giving suggestions on friendships and other relationships.

Materials:

None

© 2003
www.allsucceed.com

- Other Awareness -

HANDLING FRUSTRATIONS

Purpose: Help students learn to define and describe feelings related to personal experiences with others.

Tell the students:

> It is important that we know the way we feel about others and understand ways of explaining those feelings. This activity helps us learn ways of doing that. Please listen, follow directions, and participate.

Set aside a special place in the room for a board display entitled, Frustrations of the Day. Select a group of students to be responsible for writing serious answers to the frustration letters of their classmates. The answers could include some alternative solutions and their effects.

The frustrated person could then look at the effects of each response and choose a solution he or she considers appropriate. The board could work like this:

> On the board, have a box marked Frustrations of the Day. Students can place their frustrations in the box. Each frustration may be posted and numbered.
>
> Replies to the frustration can be placed in another box attached to the board and marked Possible Alternatives. Emphasize that the job of resolving frustrating situations is serious business and needs to be handled as such.

When possible and appropriate, suggestions may be read aloud and discussed.

Notes:

Materials:
Frustration box
 or envelope
Alternative box
 or envelope
Optional:
 Bulletin board

Notes:

- Other Awareness -

POSITIVE EXPECTATIONS

Purpose: Help students to learn and acknowledge the needs of others and to behave accordingly.

Tell the students:

> It is important that we are aware of the needs of others. This activity helps us learn more about their needs. Please listen, follow directions, and participate.

Help students see the helpful results that a positive expectation can produce. Have them role-play the suggestions below. Discuss each situation with the students for suggestions on possible actions and reactions, and then let them assume roles. It is interesting to portray both the positive and negative approach to the problem.

1. You want to play with the game at break time. Someone else has it.

2. You want to go out and play with your friends. Your mother said to clean your room first.

3. You want to go to the store with your mother. She hasn't said you could go.

4. You want to use your friend's new skates. Your friend wants to watch you, but has to do dishes first.

Ask students to determine ways of applying activity ideas to other situations.

Materials:
None

Notes:

- Other Awareness -

A BUDDY TO HELP OTHERS

Purpose: Help students learn to define and describe feelings related to personal experiences with others.

Tell the students:

> It is important that we know the way we feel about others and understand ways of explaining those feelings. This activity helps us learn ways of doing that. Please listen, follow directions, and participate.

Whenever possible, develop activities to encourage cross-age helpers. The students are encouraged to become involved with tutoring, playing games, talking, and other activities that bring together older and younger students.

This activity is very helpful in developing the quality of respect for others in both older and younger students.

Materials:

None

Notes:

- Other Awareness -

POSITIVE INTRODUCTIONS

Purpose: Help students to learn the uniqueness and differences of people.

Tell the students:

> It is important that we are aware of the uniqueness and differences of others so that we may feel happier and get along better. This activity helps us learn more about others. Please listen, follow directions, and participate.

Discuss with the class group how respecting others shows growth in maturity. One way to show respect for others is knowing how to make introductions. Ask the students to pair off and interview one another to discover unique qualities about each other.

After the interviewing is completed, ask the group to form a large circle. Taking turns, each student of the pair introduces his or her partner, stating one positive fact learned from the interview.

Proceed until everyone has been introduced.

Materials:

None

- Other Awareness -

WHICH SIDE IS BEST?

Purpose: Help students learn to define and describe feelings related to personal experiences with others.

Tell the students:

> It is important that we know the way we feel about others and understand ways of explaining those feelings. This activity helps us learn ways of doing that. Please listen, follow directions, and participate.

To demonstrate how conflicts between individuals or groups can stem from propaganda, divide the group in half and ask one-half to find articles in favor of a certain issue and the other half to find articles against it.

Ask the group to choose an issue significant to their community or one that is relevant to an issue they are studying.

Divide the board between a pro and a con side. Students who bring in articles can record on the appropriate side of the board points made in the article.

Afterward, ask students to work together to determine how the articles could affect attitudes.

Students can role-play what would happen if readers of only the pro articles began talking to readers of only the con articles. Some students could play readers of both kinds of articles and enter the argument.

After the activity, the group might be encouraged to discover methods of avoiding conflicts from reading one-sided accounts of an issue.

Notes:

Materials:

None

Notes:

- Other Awareness -

SENDING MESSAGES

Purpose: Help students learn to define and describe feelings related to personal experiences with others.

Tell the students:

It is important that we know the way we feel about others and understand ways of explaining those feelings. This activity helps us learn ways of doing that. Please listen, follow directions, and participate.

Words are only one way to send messages. Ask the students to compile a list of other ways we tell each other things. Select one or more of the examples and ask students to share as many ways as possible to send the message. Ask students to practice sending that message to others in the group.

1. Name all the ways people are told to "stop!"

2. How many individuals in the class can say, "I like you" in a way that is different from everyone else's way?

3. Describe all the ways you can think of that grown-ups use to tell you that you are bad or wrong.

4. How many ways could you ask someone else for help.

Then have students compile a list of additional examples and ways we ask and tell each other things. For each way compiled, have students determine their feelings if others send the messages to them or if they send the messages to others.

Materials:

None

 © 2003
www.allsucceed.com

- Other Awareness -

EFFECTIVE LISTENING

Purpose: Help students to learn and acknowledge the needs of others and to behave accordingly.

Tell the students:

> It is important that we are aware of the needs of others. This activity helps us learn more about their needs. Please listen, follow directions, and participate.

Have a group discussion about the importance of being an effective listener. Ask how the students feel when they say something important and no one is listening. A few volunteers may respond.

Mention that two basic ideas for effective listening are

1. look at the person who is talking, and

2. tune in to what is being said.

Students are asked to repeat these two ideas. The class is then divided into pairs consisting of a talker and a listener. The talkers repeat the basic ideas for effective listening and disclose something about themselves, such as a hobby or favorite TV show.

The listeners attempt to repeat satisfactorily what the talkers have said. The roles of talker and listener are then reversed.

If time allows, partners are changed and the exercise is repeated.

Notes:

Materials:

None

Notes:

- Other Awareness -

RELATING TO OTHERS

Purpose: Help students learn to define and describe experiences and feelings related to personal experiences with others.

Duplicate and distribute the Relating To Others activity sheet.

The following open-ended sentences might be used for group discussion, for individual conferences, or as topics for drawings or writing paragraphs or brief stories.

1. One reason that people sometimes do not understand each other is _____.

2. When I am not able to communicate with someone, I _____.

3. The way I feel about communicating is _____.

4. One way to help someone understand is _____.

Ask students to use the Creative Corner to draw or express ideas and feelings about one of their answers.

When students have completed their activity sheet, discuss the various endings with the group.

Materials:

Activity sheet

- Activity sheet -

Relating To Others

Complete the following sentences:

1. One reason that people sometimes do not understand each other is _____.

2. When I am not able to communicate with someone, _____ _____.

3. The way I feel about communicating is _____ _____.

4. One way to help someone understand is _____ _____.

Use the Creative Corner to draw or express ideas and feelings about one of your answers.

C r e a t i v e
o
r
n
e
r

Notes:

- Other Awareness -

RESPONSIBILITY FOR OTHERS' EXPERIENCES

Purpose: Help students learn to define and describe feelings related to personal experiences with others.

Tell the students:

> It is important that we know the way we feel about others and understand ways of explaining those feelings. This activity helps us learn ways of doing that. Please listen, follow directions, and participate.

To give the students the experience of being responsible for another person, start by dividing the class into two groups—A and B.

Pair a member of Group A with a member of Group B. Tell Group A that they are responsible for Group B. They will have to get out Group B's books and pencils, turn the pages for them, answer questions directed to them, and at the same time do these things for themselves. Group B is only responsible for paying attention.

After a period of time, switch responsibilities, making students in Group B the responsible ones and students in Group A the helpless ones.

After the activity is completed, have the group discuss the following:

> How did it feel to have someone else take care of your responsibilities?

Materials:

None

> Did the person handle them as well as you could have?

> Did it cause any problems? Please explain.

> How did it feel to take over someone else's problems?

Notes:

- Other Awareness -

WHAT DO YOU WISH?

Purpose: Help students to learn the uniqueness and differences of people.

Tell the students:

It is important that we are aware of the uniqueness and differences of others so that we may feel happier and get along better. This activity helps us learn more about others. Please listen, follow directions, and participate.

Have the students write and illustrate their own "I wish I were . . ." stories without signing their names.

After the stories have been written, redistribute them and have them read aloud. (If this could be embarrassing for some students because of reading or writing difficulties, read them yourself or make sure they are read by students who will not emphasize the mistakes.)

After each story is read, have the group discuss:

1. Reasons a student might wish to be what is suggested in the story.

2. What the student might do to realize the wish.

3. How realistic the expressed perception, wishes, and intentions have been illustrated.

Ask students to determine ways of applying the activity ideas to other situations.

Materials:

Drawing paper
Drawing supplies
Stapler

Notes:

- Other Awareness -

ELECTION EXPERIENCE

Purpose: Help students to learn and acknowledge the needs of others and to behave accordingly.

Tell the students:

> It is important that we are aware of the needs of others. This activity helps us learn more about their needs. Please listen, follow directions, and participate.

Hold a mock election. Choose two pairs of students to be the nominees or have the class nominate two pairs or students.

The pairs visit each student and promise to give certain rights if elected. If the rights offered by one pair mean little or nothing to the student, he or she might find those offered by the other pair more appealing. In other words, the student needs to decide which rights are most important to him or her.

After each student has been seen by each pair, hold the election. After the election, a discussion can be held to determine the reasons that one pair won over the other; that is, which rights were more important than others.

Materials:

None

© 2003
www.allsucceed.com

- Other Awareness -

HELPING EXPERIENCES

Purpose: Help students to learn and acknowledge the needs of others and to behave accordingly.

Tell the students:

> It is important that we are aware of the needs of others. This activity helps us learn more about their needs. Please listen, follow directions, and participate.

Discuss with the group a variety of things that we can do to help other people simply because they need help, not because we expect payment. If the students have trouble identifying possibilities, start them off by listing:

1. Playing with young children so that their mother can do something she has been wanting to do.

2. Reading to or playing with someone confined to bed.

3. Watering the lawn for someone on vacation.

4. Shoveling snow for someone.

Ask the students to perform such a task by a certain time.

After the time has elapsed, have them discuss their experience and their feelings about it.

Notes:

Materials:

None

Notes:

- Other Awareness -

LEARNING ABOUT SHARING

Purpose: Help students learn to define and describe feelings related to personal experiences with others.

Duplicate and distribute the Learning About Sharing activity sheet.

Ask students to complete the activity sheet and respond to such questions as:

1. What are some things your parents, brothers, sisters, teachers, or other students share with you?

2. What are some things you like to share? Please explain.

3. What are some things you do not like to share? Please explain.

4. Sharing can be fun because _____.

5. Sharing is not fun because _____.

6. Name some things people share that you cannot see.

7. Tell some other ways that you think sharing could help our classroom run better.

Materials:

Activity sheet

© 2003
www.allsucceed.com

- Activity sheet -

Learning About Sharing

Please complete the following:

1. What are some things your parents, brothers, sisters, teachers, or other students share with you?

2. What are some things you like to share? Please explain.

3. What are some things you do not like to share? Please explain.

4. Sharing can be fun because _____.

5. Sharing is not fun because _____.

6. Name some things people share that you cannot see.

7. Tell some other ways that you think sharing could help our classroom run better.

Notes:

- Other Awareness -

POSITIVE FEEDBACK

Purpose: Help students to learn the uniqueness and differences of people.

Tell the students:

> It is important that we are aware of the uniqueness and differences of others so that we may feel happier and get along better. This activity helps us learn more about others. Please listen, follow directions, and participate.

Discuss with the group how people are all different but that there are positive traits in all of us.

Put the name of everyone in the class on separate slips of paper and put them in a container. Ask each student to draw a name, one at a time.

When the student draws a name, he or she tells something he or she likes about that person.

This encourages students to respect others and provides an opportunity for all to find and hear positive things about them.

Ask students to determine the effects that hearing this positive information may have on:
1. friendships
2. feelings of self-worth
3. respect for other people

Ask students to determine other ways of applying activity ideas.

Materials:

Slips of paper
Container

 © 2003
www.allsucceed.com

- Other Awareness -

LEADERSHIP

Purpose: Help students learn to define and describe feelings related to personal experiences with others.

Tell the students:

It is important that we know the way we feel about others and understand ways of explaining those feelings. This activity helps us learn ways of doing that. Please listen, follow directions, and participate.

Many leaders in the world are men. When a mixed group of men and women get together, a male may be chosen to be the chairperson or the president. This activity touches on the issue of leadership and women. Divide the students into groups of four, mixing boys or men and girls or women in each group and tell them the following:

Your group has two tasks to complete. A boy or man is to be the group leader for task one and a girl or woman for task two. Take only 10 minutes for each task; appoint someone to watch the time. Go as far as you can with each task.

Task one: Write a list of three or more reasons for supporting the nomination of a woman for the next election for president. Number the reasons to show the order in which each reason is likely to be convincing.

Task two: Write a list of three or more changes that have occurred in work or in society that have encouraged some women to seek more equality with men. Then number the changes to show their importance.

Have a group discussion about what they have learned about leadership and women after the tasks are completed.

Notes:

Materials:

None
Optional:
　Reference
　Information

Notes:

- Other Awareness -

PEOPLE INFORMATION

Purpose: Help students to learn the uniqueness and differences of people.

Duplicate and distribute the People Information activity sheet.

At the top of each square, ask students to write the name of another student in your group. In the big part of the square put:

1. A √ if the person likes to play the same kinds of games you do.
2. A □ if the person does about the same kind of work in school as you do.
3. An ✕ if the person lives on your block.
4. A ∆ if you would like to invite that person to your house to eat dinner.
5. A ○ if you would like that person to play on your team or with you.

Example:

Bob
∆ ○ ✕

Discuss with the students the information they gathered. Do all the boxes look the same? Please explain.

Materials:

Activity sheet

- Activity sheet -

People Information

At the top of each square, put the name of another student in your group. In the big part of the square put:

1. A √ if the person likes to play the same kinds of games you do.

2. A ☐ if the person does about the same kind of work in school as you do.

3. An ✕ if the person lives on your block.

4. A ∆ if you would like to invite that person to your house to eat dinner.

5. A ○ if you would like that person to play on your team or with you.

Example:

Bob
∆ ○ ✕

Notes:

- Other Awareness -

MYSTERY FRIEND

Purpose: Help students to learn and acknowledge the needs of others and to behave accordingly.

Tell the students:

It is important that we are aware of the needs of others. This activity helps us learn more about their needs. Please listen, follow directions, and participate.

Discuss ways of showing friendship to each other in the room. Ask students to think of as many new ideas as possible. List their ideas on the board.

Ask students to put their names on pieces of paper for a drawing. Ask four volunteers to draw names.

Tell the volunteers the following:

The slip of paper you have just drawn contains the name of your mystery friend for the day. You are not to tell whose name you have, but during the day you are to do three or four friendly things for that person because he or she is your mystery friend for the day. At the end of the day, I'll ask you to tell us who your mystery friend is and what you did.

Near the end of the day, ask the four volunteers to reveal the names of their mystery friends. Ask each volunteer to explain things they did for their mystery friend and how they felt doing those things.

Ask each friend the following:

Did you know you were a mystery friend?
How did you find out?
How did you feel?

Repeat the activity so that everyone has an opportunity to be and to treat a mystery friend. Ask students to determine ways of applying the ideas generated from this activity to other situations.

Materials:

Slips of paper

- Other Awareness -

STUDENT SING-A-LONG

Purpose: Help students learn the uniqueness and differences of people.

Tell the students:

It is important that we are aware of the uniqueness and differences of others so that we may feel happier and get along better. This activity helps us learn more about others. Please listen, follow directions, and participate.

Ask the students to use the melody of the song, *Mary Had A Little Lamb*, and improvise some words that point up a positive characteristic of someone in the group. Sing a verse such as "Mary has a lot of friends." The students guess who the student is and then sing it back, inserting the student's name.

Example:
   Peter has a lot of friends.

Some possible verses:

   Someone always shares his toys.
   Someone has a lot of friends.
   Someone is a hard worker.
   Someone is a dependable helper.
   Someone is a friendly person.
   Someone is a deep thinker.
   Someone never shoves in line.
   Someone always sings so happily.
   Someone takes turns very well.
   Someone learned to tie his shoes.

Students may want to write their own melody and positive characteristic lyrics and teach the song to the group.

Notes:

Materials:

None

Notes:

- Other Awareness -

THE HELPFUL WAY TO SAY IT GAME

Purpose: Help students learn to define and describe feelings related to personal experiences with others.

Tell the students:

> It is important that we know the way we feel about others and understand ways of explaining those feelings. This activity helps us learn ways of doing that. Please listen, follow directions, and participate.

Let the students role-play the helpful way to tell someone and the hurtful way to tell someone:

> to help you do something
>
> that he or she is not to play in a certain way
>
> that you don't want to play or get together today
>
> that he or she is not playing or acting fairly

Students may think of additional activities. Ask students to determine their feelings toward the other people in each example. Ask students to determine how helpful and hurtful ways of telling effects getting along with others.

Ask students to determine various applications to the ideas generated from this activity.

Materials:

None

© 2003
www.allsucceed.com

Notes:

- Other Awareness -

ACKNOWLEDGING OTHERS

Purpose: Help students to learn the uniqueness and differences of people.

Duplicate this page of positive phrases, cut the phrases apart, and distribute them to the class.

Ask each student to give his or her phrase to persons the phrases describe. Since all statements are positive, each person could have some feelings of achievement and recognition. The students may share their phrases and tell what behaviors encouraged them to present a particular phrase to a particular person.

Excels in sports	Is always happy
Enjoys helping others	Smiles at everyone
Is an effective listener	Is a reliable friend
Has a fun sense of humor	Is an effective leader
Handles responsibility	Never gives up
Does well in art	Is dependable
Says kind things about others	

Materials:

Duplicated page

Notes:

- Other Awareness -

INTERDEPENDENCE

Purpose: Help students to learn the uniqueness and differences of people.

Tell the students:

> It is important that we are aware of the uniqueness and differences of others so that we may feel happier and get along better. This activity helps us learn more about others. Please listen, follow directions, and participate.

Ask students to name an item, such as a newspaper or a carton of milk, that is common to their way of life.

Ask students to think about all the people it takes to get the named item from its beginning to their homes.

Write on the board all the responses given by the class.

When the lists are complete, erase just one of the categories named, like delivery person, and have the class discuss what would happen if just one person in the entire process did not do his or her job.

Ask students to discuss the following:

1. What is important about the job?

2. Explain the way interdependence fits in work situations.

3. Explain the way interdependence relates to a family.

4. Explain the way interdependence relates to relationships with other students.

Ask students to determine other applications of ideas generated from this activity.

Materials:
None

 © 2003
www.allsucceed.com

38

Notes:

- Other Awareness -

UNDERSTANDING NEED BLOCKS

Purpose: Help students to learn and acknowledge the needs of others and to behave accordingly.

Tell the students:

It is important that we are aware of the needs of others. This activity helps us learn more about their needs. Please listen, follow directions, and participate.

Analyze specific situations by describing the needs and determining which factors are blocking having those needs met. This activity may be done in small groups or in a large group.

Sample Chart

Situation   **Needs**   **What is Blocking Needs**

Determine the needs and what is blocking the needs in each of the following situations:

Jim has been getting into fights with all of the boys in this class. He has no one to play with at home or at school.

Sally was having trouble concentrating on her work. She had not eaten any breakfast and had gone to bed late the night before.

Make up other situations as appropriate with the group.

Ask the students to give situation suggestions based on their experiences.

Materials:

None

Notes:

- Other Awareness -

SUPER SPORTSMANSHIP

Purpose: Help students to learn and acknowledge the needs of others and to behave accordingly.

Tell the students:

    It is important that we are aware of the needs of others. This activity helps us learn more about their needs. Please listen, follow directions, and participate.

Discuss with your class group the meaning of "super sportsmanship."

Examples include:

        playing fair

        sharing equipment

        being a "super" winner

        being a "super" loser

        taking turns

        not hurting the feelings of others

Have the students draw cartoons illustrating one example of super sportsmanship and discuss it with the class.

Materials:

Drawing paper
Drawing supplies

Notes:

- Other Awareness -

UNDERSTANDING INTERPRETATION DIFFERENCES

Purpose: Help students to learn the uniqueness and differences of people.

Tell the students:

> It is important that we are aware of the uniqueness and differences of others so that we may feel happier and get along better. This activity helps us learn more about others. Please listen, follow directions, and participate.

Conflicts often develop from different interpretations of a single situation or event. In some cases interpretations can reflect individual interests. One interpretation is not more valid than another.

People can avoid conflict by learning to recognize and tolerate irreconcilable differences in others. Illustrate by preparing a series of pictures for a contest. Some pictures might show familiar animals or objects. Others could be ambiguous—for example, ink blots or prints of modern art. As the pictures are shown, the students record what they see.

When the students review the pictures aloud, challenge their answers. Dictionaries, textbooks, the Internet, and other information sources can be used to prove their answers for the familiar pictures, but a debate might seem necessary to determine which answers are correct for the ambiguous pictures.

During this activity, encourage students to see that one answer is not more correct than another and that further argument is therefore futile.

Answers for the remaining pictures might simply be enjoyed for their variety.

Materials:

Pictures of familiar animals and objects
Ambiguous pictures

Notes:

- Other Awareness -

THE RIGHTS OF OTHERS

Purpose: Help students to learn and acknowledge the needs of others and to behave accordingly.

Duplicate and distribute The Rights of Others activity sheet.

Ask students to complete the following activity sheet:

1. One right that is important to me is _____.

2. It is important to me because _____.

3. To me, respect for the rights of others means _____.

4. One thing that causes problems about respecting the rights of others is _____.

Ask students to draw or express additional thoughts and feelings in the Creative Corner.

After all students are finished, they may volunteer to read their endings and give their reasons for choosing those endings.

Materials:

Activity sheet

- Activity sheet -

The Rights of Others

Complete the following sentences:

1. One right that is important to me is _____ _____.

2. It is important to me because _____ _____.

3. To me, respect for the rights of others means _____ _____.

4. One thing that causes problems about respecting the rights of others is _____.

Draw or express additional thoughts and feelings in the Creative Corner.

```
Creative
o
r
n
e
r
```

43

Notes:

- Other Awareness -

BUDDY BUSINESS

Purpose: Help students to learn and acknowledge the needs of others and to behave accordingly.

Tell the students:

It is important that we are aware of the needs of others. These activities help us learn ways to know. Please listen, follow directions, and participate.

Activities related to responsibility that utilize the use of buddy partners might include:
1. Discussion between buddies on responsibility:
   What it means to each buddy.
   How important it is to each of them.
   How older and younger students differ in their ability to handle it.
   What responsibility each buddy feels he or she has toward the other.
   Problems they might be having in terms of responsibility to each other.
   How these might be worked out.

2. Consideration of the phrase, "my brother's keeper."
   What it means and where it originated.
   What are some different feelings about it?

3. Setting up a project of any type that would require each buddy to take some responsibility for its completion. All pairs of buddies could meet and decide on types of projects to take on, or each pair could decide on their own.

4. Meeting of all pairs of buddies to discuss responsibility and what each pair thought and did about accepting it.

Materials:

None

- Other Awareness -

WHAT ARE MY RIGHTS?

Purpose: Help students to learn and acknowledge the needs and rights of others and to behave accordingly.

Tell the students:

> It is important that we are aware of the needs and rights of others. This activity helps us learn more about their needs. Please listen, follow directions, and participate.

Discuss with the group the fact that everyone has rights. Read the Bill of Rights or some similar document applicable to all people. Assign for completion an open-ended sentence:

> People forget about my rights when they _____
> _____
> _____.

Ask students to read and discuss the completed sentences and suggest what can be done when the rights of others are forgotten.

Notes:

Materials:

Optional:
Bill of Rights

Notes:

- Other Awareness -

RESPONSIBILITIES

Purpose: Help students learn to define and describe feelings related to responsibility and personal experiences with others.

Tell the students:

> It is important that we know the way we feel about others and understand the part responsibility plays. This activity helps us learn ways of doing that. Please listen, follow directions, and participate.

Ask each student to suggest a responsibility for group behavior and explain the reason it would be important to adopt the responsibility for the group.

Next, ask each student to suggest one responsibility that would not be appropriate and explain the reason.

Then discuss whether the latter responsibility could be changed to make it better.

Ask the students to determine the way improvements can be made to the responsibilities.

Ask students to determine ways of applying their ideas to life situations. Ask them to identify their feelings as a result of being responsible.

Materials:

None

© 2003
www.allsucceed.com

- Other Awareness -

FEELING SITUATIONS

Purpose: Help students learn to define and describe feelings related to personal experiences with others.

Tell the students:

> It is important that we know the way we feel about others and understand ways of explaining those feelings. This activity helps us learn ways of doing that. Please listen, follow directions, and participate.

Have students number papers from 1 to 4 and write feelings for each situation.

1. Linda works very hard at school and spends many hours going over her work to make sure that her answers are correct. Today, she got her math paper back and the problem she did for extra credit was marked wrong. She couldn't believe it! How does Linda feel?

2. Aaron likes to play baseball. He played in all of the school games and scored runs in almost every game. He was voted "Most Outstanding Player." How does he feel?

3. Anita's mother taught her how to sew. She made some new pants and a shirt to wear to school. Several girls told Anita that she was wearing the best-looking outfit in school. How does Anita feel?

4. Jay works hard and does well in school. The final exam in math is today. It seems as if the teacher has made it hard. It seems too long to finish before the bell rings. Jay begins to tremble and perspire. How does Jay feel?

Discuss the feeling responses with the group. Ask the group to determine ways to apply the activity ideas to other situations.

Notes:

Materials:

Optional: Feeling Words Cards beginning on page 296

Notes:

- Other Awareness -

HANDLING DIFFERENT OPINIONS

Purpose: Help students to learn the uniqueness and differences of people.

Tell the students:

> It is important that we are aware of the uniqueness and differences of others so that we may feel happier and get along better. This activity helps us learn more about others. Please listen, follow directions, and participate.

Discuss with the students the ways people differ in opinions and how the opinions of others are worthy of understanding and respect.

Then direct every class member to complete the following open-ended sentence:

> The book (program, sport, etc.) I like best is_____
> _____.

Have volunteers read their complete sentence to the class and then discuss individual opinions and tell the reason each is worthy of respect.

Materials:

None

- Other Awareness -

EMOTIONAL MATURITY

Purpose: Help students learn to define and describe feelings related to personal experiences with others.

Tell the students:

> It is important that we know the way we feel about others and understand ways of explaining those feelings. This activity helps us learn ways of doing that. Please listen, follow directions, and participate.

Have a discussion about growing emotionally as well as physically. Emphasize ways that consideration for other people's feelings helps us emotionally.

Read an incident from a book or story that reveals how a character showed consideration for the feelings of another and thereby demonstrated emotional growth.

Use an appropriate book or other literature that is included in your curriculum for your example.

Discuss the situation with the students and determine ways the example may relate to them.

Notes:

Materials:

None

Notes:

- Other Awareness -

PROBLEM BOX SUPPORT

Purpose: Help students learn to define and describe feelings related to personal experiences with others.

Tell the students:

> It is important that we know the way we feel about others and understand ways of explaining those feelings. This activity helps us learn ways of doing that. Please listen, follow directions, and participate

Explain this idea as follows:

> All of us from time to time have problems that bother us. Or perhaps we know of a problem that is bothering somebody else. All of us would like to help and give advice about the problem. That is the reason we have the Problem Box. At any time, you may write out a problem that is bothering you and that you would like some help on and slip it into the box. You need not sign the paper. Then, from time to time, I will take a problem out of the box and share it with the class for their thinking. This is your opportunity to share your problems, to have them discussed without anyone knowing that it is your problem. Any questions?

Encourage questions so that the students may be very clear about the purpose of the Problem Box.

If students would like to sign their names but remain anonymous to the other students, be sure to keep that information private. The student who signs his or her name indicates that that is the intention.

Materials:

Box

- Other Awareness -

SECURITY WITH OTHERS

Purpose: Help students learn to define and describe feelings related to personal experiences with others.

Tell the students:

> It is important that we know the way we feel about others and understand ways of explaining those feelings. This activity helps us learn ways of doing that. Please listen, follow directions, and participate.

Discuss with the class ways to feel secure and comfortable with others.

<u>Without mentioning names</u>, have volunteers tell something they find helpful and something they find hurtful about their peers' behaviors.

Discuss ideas for handling hurtful behavior so students feel secure. Ask students to give alternative helpful behavior suggestions.

Ask students to determine the effect the different behaviors have on friendships and other relationships.

Notes:

Materials:

None

Notes:

- Other Awareness -

SPREAD THE JOY

Purpose: Help students learn to define and describe feelings related to personal experiences with others.

Tell the students:

> It is important that we know the way we feel about others and understand ways of explaining those feelings. This activity helps us learn ways of doing that. Please listen, follow directions, and participate.

Emotions tend to be infectious. For example, when you smile at someone the person often smiles back and feels even better. Sometimes, crying people sadden or depress those around them. Each student might be asked to smile at someone, encourage someone to laugh, or cheer someone up during after-school hours or break time.

The students could demonstrate or describe either in writing or orally not only what happened, but also how they felt after they shared a happy feeling with someone else.

This can also be used in eliciting other pleasant emotional responses.

Materials:

None

© 2003
www.allsucceed.com

Notes:

- Other Awareness -

DEVELOPING POSITIVE HUMAN RELATIONS

Purpose: Help students to learn and acknowledge the needs of others and to behave accordingly.

Tell the students:

> It is important that we are aware of the needs of others. This activity helps us learn more about their needs. Please listen, follow directions, and participate.

Discuss with the class group the meaning of human relationships. Include brotherhood, freedom from prejudice, and stereotyping.

Ask students to brainstorm a list of human relations examples.

Divide the students into small groups and have each group role-play episodes showing helpful and hurtful human relationships in appropriate situations.

Ask students to discuss the behavior choices in the role-play and the impact those choices had on the relationships in the role-play.

Ask students to determine ways to apply the ideas generated from this activity to various situations.

Materials:

None

Notes:

- Other Awareness -

APPLYING THE DEFINITION OF AVERAGE

Purpose: Help students learn the uniqueness and differences of people.

Tell the students:

It is important that we are aware of the uniqueness and differences of others so that we may feel happier and get along better. This activity helps us learn more about others. Please listen, follow directions, and participate.

The word *average* is misused by many people, and, consequently, many other people understand themselves by seeing how they compare with the "average" person. To help better understand what this word really means, ask the following question:

Have many of you ever met the average person?

Then follow with these questions:

What does the average person look like?
How smart is the person?
How many friends does the person have?
What does the person feel about his or her school, home, and so on?

Ask the students to answer these questions. Once they have an assessment of the average person in the group, discuss how valid their kind of assessment is, whether it is important for them to know what the average is, and the reasons. Remind the students that an average is always defined by and bound to a context; this context happens to be the group. A person who is not average in this group might be average in another. An *average* refers not to a person but to an estimate.

Explain this concept to the group.

Materials:
None

- Other Awareness -

IDENTIFY THE MYSTERY PERSON

Purpose: Help students learn the uniqueness and differences of people.

Tell the students:

> It is important that we are aware of the uniqueness and differences of others so that we may feel happier and get along better. This activity helps us learn more about others. Please listen, follow directions, and participate.

Each student can take a turn being a mystery person.

The mystery person could be an important part of the other students' lives, responsible for their health or welfare, or for some service to them; the person could be a doctor, a teacher, a senator, or a mail carrier.

For a slightly different emphasis, the mystery person might be a person from their history, geography, or reading lesson; an Australian Aborigine responsible for the tribe; or Admiral Byrd, responsible for his expedition to the South Pole.

The mystery person gives the group clues to his or her identity, one clue at a time.

The clues will reveal what the student feels that person is responsible for.

After each clue, the group might explain whom or what he represents. Have a discussion after the mystery person is identified to see if the other students felt that the person's responsibilities were brought out in the clues.

Notes:

Materials:
None

Notes:

- Other Awareness -

EXPRESSIONS ABOUT OTHERS

Purpose: Help students learn the uniqueness and differences of people.

Tell the students:

> It is important that we are aware of the uniqueness and differences of others so that we may feel happier and get along better. This activity helps us learn more about others. Please listen, follow directions, and participate.

This activity can be done in small groups or with the entire class. Ask one student to select a fellow student (in his or her mind). Then, ask each student to ask a question to determine who the person is and have the person respond with a head nod or short answer after each question.

At that time, the others in the group would guess who he or she is thinking of.

Possible questions:

> What kind of car would this person be?
> What article of clothing?
> What street sign?
> If he were a light bulb, how many watts would he be?
> What color would he be?
> What kind of fruit?
> What animal?
> What material? Piece of furniture? Dessert? Game? Actor or Actress?

It is important that students state the way they see the person being. For example, not this person likes the color green, but what color the other student sees him as being. When the person is guessed, the students can discuss the reasons each student saw him as such; if the other students see him in the same or different terms; and how the student sees himself.

Materials:
None

- Other Awareness -

THE IMPACT OF SMILING

Purpose: Help students learn the uniqueness and differences of people.

Tell the students:

> It is important that we are aware of the uniqueness and differences of others so that we may feel happier and get along better. This activity helps us learn more about others. Please listen, follow directions, and participate.

Ask the students to cut out various smiles from magazines. Together, make a collage using the caption, "Smiles are for everyone."

Discuss how people's smiles are different. Continue with how people show happy feelings in different ways.

The students may volunteer to tell the group how they show their happy feelings.

Notes:

Materials:

Magazines
Scissors

Notes:

- Other Awareness -

UNDERSTANDING YOUR NEEDS

Purpose: Help students to learn and acknowledge the needs of others and to behave accordingly.

Tell the students:

> It is important that we are aware of the needs of others. This activity helps us learn ways to know that. Please listen, follow directions, and participate.

Have the students identify, discuss, and define human needs. This definition may be written on the board: a *need* is a lack of something which is essential, desirable, or useful.

Further discussion can delve into:

1. How people satisfy their needs.

2. Differences in the methods used to satisfy needs.

3. Constructive and nonconstructive ways to meet needs.

4. Explain the reasons people might choose a different method.

5. Explain the reason the same method of satisfying a need isn't successful for all people.

Students' suggestions on the meaning of *needs* may also be written on the board. Discussion may follow any new meanings suggested by the class.

Materials:

None

Notes:

- Other Awareness -

THE IMPACT OF THE BILL OF RIGHTS

Purpose: Help students to learn and acknowledge the rights of others and to behave accordingly.

Tell the students:

It is important that we are aware of the needs of others. This activity helps us learn more about their needs. Please listen, follow directions, and participate.

Discuss the Bill of Rights with the group. The discussion could concern some of the following questions:

1. Were the amendments in the Bill of Rights important to the people at the time they were written?
2. Explain the reason they felt it necessary to add the amendments to the Constitution.
3. Are they important now?
4. Which rights in the Bill of Rights are most important to you? Please explain.

Can you think of any problems these rights could cause? For example:

1. A newspaper wants to print instructions on how to make a bomb.
2. Some people want to hold meetings to plan a campaign to have the President of the U.S. impeached.
3. A college president wants to post soldiers around his campus.
4. A newscaster wants to exercise his freedom of speech on TV.

Are there examples of times when you feel people need to be allowed to demand certain rights? Are there any examples of times when people do not need to be allowed to demand rights?

Materials:

The Bill of Rights

© 2003
www.allsucceed.com

Notes:

- Other Awareness -

PREJUDICE OR FACT?

Purpose: Help students learn the difference between fact and prejudice and its impact on relationship.

Duplicate and distribute the Prejudice or Fact? activity sheet. In the blank provided, write **P** if the statement is prejudiced, **NP** if the statement is not prejudiced, or **CD** if you cannot decide.

_____ 1. She's the one who stole the candy. See the chocolate on her mouth?

_____ 2. He will flunk the test. He usually does.

_____ 3. She has blond hair and blue eyes.

_____ 4. Look at the way he dresses. He must be poor.

_____ 5. I know you'll like her. She's pretty.

_____ 6. Don't play with her. She looks funny.

_____ 7. He can really catch a ball. He has big hands.

_____ 8. Oh, don't choose him. He's too smart.

_____ 9. Of course he was cheating. His book was open, wasn't it?

_____ 10. She is very sly. Look how her eyes are slanted.

Write the definition of *prejudice* on the board (see dictionary). After the students have completed the activity sheet, discuss their answers and the reasons they were chosen.

Materials:

Activity sheet

© 2003
www.allsucceed.com

- Activity sheet -

Prejudice Or Fact?

In the blank provided, write **P** if the statement is <u>prejudiced</u>, **NP** if the statement is <u>not prejudiced,</u> or **CD** if you <u>cannot decide</u>.

____ 1. She's the one who stole the candy. See the chocolate on her mouth?

____ 2. He will flunk the test. He usually does.

____ 3. She has blond hair and blue eyes.

____ 4. Look at the way he dresses. He must be poor.

____ 5. I know you'll like her. She's pretty.

____ 6. Don't play with her. She looks funny.

____ 7. He can really catch a ball. He has big hands.

____ 8. Oh, don't choose him. He's too smart.

____ 9. Of course he was cheating. His book was open, wasn't it?

____ 10. She is very sly. Look how her eyes are slanted.

Notes:

- Other Awareness -

BULLYING ROLE-PLAY

Purpose: Help students to learn and acknowledge the needs of others and to behave accordingly.

Tell the students:

> It is important that we are aware of the needs of others. This activity helps us learn more about their needs. Please listen, follow directions, and participate.

Have a group discussion about the problem of bullying. Ask the students to role-play the following situations:

1. The students had all made posters advertising their class play. They were going to vote on the best poster. The best poster would be placed in the school office. Maria knew that her poster was not as well done as some of the others, but she told all the girls if they did not vote for her poster she would not invite them to her party.

2. Juan had a new bike. It was his first mountain bike. He rode it over to his friend Tom's house to show it to him. Tom looked at the bike and said, "It's okay, but it isn't nearly as good as mine," and grabbed the bike. Juan fell off.

3. Jerry had a candy bar in his lunch bag. Chen, who was much larger then Jerry, wanted it. He told Jerry to give it to him or "I pity you when we get out of school today!"

Discuss using the following questions:

1. How do you feel about the bully? Please explain.

2. Give the reasons some people seem to enjoy behaving this way.

3. What can you do about people like this?

Materials:

None

© 2003
www.allsucceed.com

- Other Awareness -

GIVING AND RECEIVING RESPECT

Purpose: Help students learn the uniqueness and differences of people.

Tell the students:

> It is important that we are aware of the uniqueness and differences of others so that we may feel happier and get along better. This activity helps us learn more about others. Please listen, follow directions, and participate.

Discuss with the group ways that students could recognize themselves as a unique person, worthy of self-respect as well as respect from others. Collect pictures of students and arrange them on a board or around the room.

Have students examine the arrangement of pictures and discuss the similarities and differences in the group.

Relate the ideas generated from this activity to other situations.

Notes:

Materials:

Photos of students

Notes:

- Other Awareness -

PROMOTING UNDERSTANDING

Purpose: Help students learn the uniqueness and differences of people.

Tell the students:

> It is important that we are aware of the uniqueness and differences of others so that we may feel happier and get along better. This activity helps us learn more about others. Please listen, follow directions, and participate.

Discuss with the students the reason it is important to gain insight into others in order to understand them. Ask students to find pictures of people in magazines showing interest in another's activities and create a collage with them.

Then, discuss with the group how sharing interests promotes understanding of others.

Ask each student to explain his or her collage.

Ask students to determine ways of applying activity ideas to life situations.

Materials:

Magazines
Collage materials

- Other Awareness -

GROUP INTERESTS

Purpose: Help students learn the uniqueness and differences of people.

Tell the students:

> It is important that we are aware of the uniqueness and differences of others so that we may feel happier and get along better. This activity helps us learn more about others. Please listen, follow directions, and participate.

Have a discussion about the interests and differences of others, emphasizing that learning about others enriches us.

Tell a story of students, one who grew up in the inner city and the other on a farm. Use lead questions to elicit from the students that one's environmental background is a factor in determining individual interests and differences.

Show the group magazine pictures or Internet sites illustrating diversified interests. Develop a book with a taped commentary of each picture, giving possible reasons for individual interests of students.

At a class center, allow each student to draw an interest and explain it on the tape.

Put the drawings together in book form and coordinate them with the tape.

Use the tape again as a listening center, allowing students to review the interests of each student in the class by listening to the tape while viewing the individual interest book.

Notes:

Materials:

Magazines
Construction paper
Art supplies
Tape recorder

Notes:

- Other Awareness -

I'M A COMPUTER

Purpose: Help students learn the uniqueness and differences of people.

Tell the students:

It is important that we are aware of the uniqueness and differences of others so that we may feel happier and get along better. This activity helps us learn more about others. Please listen, follow directions, and participate.

Read the following poem to the class:

> I'm a computer,
> You're a computer.
> I'm full of ideas,
> Think what I know!
>
> You're a computer,
> I'm a computer.
> You're full of ideas,
> What do you know?
> —T. R. Radd

When the poem has been read, help students understand what is meant by "I am a computer," and "you are a computer." Discuss the part of the body that is similar to a computer.

Help your students choose a partner. Then ask them to draw their partner's picture. Ask each partner to draw objects or situations that record how the person they are drawing appears to them. They do not have to draw a picture of what the other person looks like. As an example, if a student is very kind, gentle, and courteous, then the student recording would draw pictures that record the traits they see in the other person. Have them explain what they see in each other to each other.

Materials:
Drawing paper
Drawing supplies

© 2003
www.allsucceed.com

Notes:

- Other Awareness -

DESCRIBING OTHERS

Purpose: Help students learn the uniqueness and differences of people.

Tell the students:

> It is important that we are aware of the uniqueness and differences of others so that we may feel happier and get along better. This activity helps us learn more about others. Please listen, follow directions, and participate.

Ask the students to close their eyes. Then, choose one student to leave the room. After the student has left, the students open their eyes. Tell them who has left and have them describe as many things as they can remember about him or her. A possible variation is to give a description of someone in your group and let the students guess whom you are describing.

Some possible ideas to discuss with the class are:

1. What would happen if the information describing the student who left applied to the whole group? Would you be able to guess who was out of the room?

2. Discuss several reasons it is often helpful that information describing each person be different.

Ask students to relate the ideas from this activity to other situations.

Materials:

None

Notes:

- Other Awareness -

WHO ARE YOU? GAME

Purpose: Help students learn the uniqueness and differences of people.

Tell the students:

> It is important that we are aware of the uniqueness and differences of others so that we may feel happier and get along better. This activity helps us learn more about others. Please listen, follow directions, and participate.

Discuss with the students ways of distinguishing characteristics of each student in the class.

Describe one of the students in the class, emphasizing only positive qualities.

Let the other students guess the student's identity.

When the students have the idea of how to give the description, let them give the clues about someone.

Begin with physical characteristics and gradually shift to other characteristics.

Discuss ways we can remember and work with others because of our positive qualities.

Materials:

None

 © 2003
www.allsucceed.com

Notes:

- Other Awareness -

BEHAVIOR SURPRISE

Purpose: Help students to learn and acknowledge the needs of others and to behave accordingly.

Tell the students:

It is important that we are aware of the needs of others. This activity helps us learn more about their needs. Please listen, follow directions, and participate.

Enlist the aid of a student to act as a confederate in an experiment. The selection of a student who will remain confidential is important to the success of this activity. Also, the student needs to be carefully selected and not be threatened by the role. The student needs to be well known and respected in the group.

Instruct the student to act in an entirely different manner from the usual. For example, a normally attentive and cooperative student who is interested in school and participates readily in activities might be unruly, boisterous, and disruptive and balk at participating in anything.

It is important that the student behave so differently that all the students will notice. At the end of the day, the confederate can admit the experiment and a discussion can be held regarding the unusual behavior and the reactions the class had to it. Discuss these questions:

Do people really have set traits?

What are the advantages and disadvantages of set traits?

Explain ways people can choose to improve and change.

Materials:

None

Notes:

- Other Awareness -

MAGIC GIFT

Purpose: Help students learn the uniqueness and differences of people.

Tell the students:

It is important that we are aware of the uniqueness and differences of others so that we may feel happier and get along better. This activity helps us learn more about others. Please listen, follow directions, and participate.

Ask students to reveal some of their inner differences—aspects of themselves that are not outwardly apparent. You will need a magic wand or a pretend wand. Have each student describe him or herself. Then read the following poem to the students about the magic wand.

> Just in time I got a gift
> That really gave me quite a lift—
> A magic wand that clearly shows
> My thoughts and feelings that I don't know.
> Swish, the magic wand reveals all of me,
> Showing all the great things I'd like to be.
> Now, that special self I see rarely shows
> So how could anyone else ever know?
> I seldom see myself this way,
> Have you? I want to hear what you have to say.
> —T. R. Radd

Make sure that students understand the idea of the magic wand.

Materials:

Read the first four lines again.

Optional:
Wand

Ask students to swish their magic wand and tell something about themselves. For instance, "Tell us about a time when you felt happy." Accept all answers.

Notes:

- Other Awareness -

A POSITIVE FOCUS

Purpose: Help students learn the uniqueness and differences of people and the effect of focusing on the helpful qualities of others.

Tell the students:

> It is important that we are aware of the uniqueness and differences of others so that we may feel happier and get along better. This activity helps us learn more about others. Please listen, follow directions, and participate.

Discuss with the students the importance of looking for the helpful qualities in others. Explain that looking for the helpful qualities in others can bring out the best in other people and themselves.

Discuss with the class the outward behavior of persons who consistently see the helpful qualities in others, then contrast their behavior with the behavior of those who do not make this effort. Explain the positive effects on people's behavior and feelings when they have a positive focus about other persons.

Ask students to think of examples of times they had a positive focus and saw the helpful qualities in others. Please do not mention names.

Discuss the ways looking for the helpful qualities in others affects friendship.

Ask students to determine ways of applying activity ideas to life situations.

Materials:

None

Notes:

- Other Awareness -

THE POWER OF HUMOR

Purpose: Help students learn to define and describe feelings related to personal experiences with others.

Tell the students:

> It is important that we know the way we feel about others and understand ways of explaining those feelings. This activity helps us learn ways of doing that. Please listen, follow directions, and participate.

To encourage humor as a viable means of expression, suggest that the group have a joke-telling session to be carried on at different times throughout the year.

Members of the group could bring in their favorite jokes—the ones that are the funniest. After each joke is told, the students can rate it, giving it five points if they found it very funny and zero points if they did not find it funny at all. A discussion could follow about both the joke and the reasons some students found it funny while others did not.

A general discussion could bring out how the class feels about humor, whether it is important to them, and how important it is.

Joke telling might be incorporated into different student projects, such as the student-of-the-week activity.

Materials:

Jokes from students

www.allsucceed.com

- Other Awareness -

GROUP INFORMATION SEARCH

Purpose: Help students learn the uniqueness and differences of people.

Tell the students:

> It is important that we are aware of the uniqueness and differences of others so that we may feel happier and get along better. This activity helps us learn more about others. Please listen, follow directions, and participate.

Use a series of questions beginning with "How many of you . . .?"

Examples:

enjoy playing baseball?

listen to music by Bach?

enjoy cooking?

like to paint?

weight 90 pounds?

have brown hair?

have blue eyes?

Students can add other categories as appropriate.

Record how many students raise their hands for each question. This would point out that similarities and differences exist within the group.

Discuss each question to ascertain the reasons certain students raised their hands and others did not.

Notes:

Materials:

None

Notes:

- Other Awareness -

GROUP UNIQUENESS

Purpose: Help students learn the uniqueness and differences of people.

Tell the students:

> It is important that we are aware of the uniqueness and differences of others so that we may feel happier and get along better. This activity helps us learn more about others. Please listen, follow directions, and participate.

With group participation, make a list of all of the things that are unique to the individuals in the group, stressing only positive attributes. Then have the students discuss the importance of each other's uniqueness.

Discuss how all groups are unique, just like all individuals are unique.

Ask students to determine ways of applying the activity ideas to other situations.

Materials:

None

- Other Awareness -

USING OUR IMAGINATIONS

Purpose: Help students learn to define and describe feelings related to personal experiences with others.

Tell the students:

> It is important that we know the way we feel about others and understand ways of explaining those feelings. This activity helps us learn ways of doing that. Please listen, follow directions, and participate.

Discuss with the students the importance of expressing ideas and respecting the ideas of others, no matter how extreme they may seem.

Let the students start with the words, "Just imagine . . ." and express any ideas that occur to them. For example, just imagine:

1. that we are dolphins instead of people.

2. that we had wings and could fly to every place we talk about in school.

3. that we could choose our own teachers.

Ask students to determine ways to apply the ideas from the activity to other situations.

Notes:

Materials:

None

Notes:

- Other Awareness -

SPECIAL IDENTITY EXPERIENCE

Purpose: Help students learn the uniqueness and differences of people.

Tell the students:

> It is important that we are aware of the uniqueness and differences of others so that we may feel happier and get along better. This activity helps us learn more about others. Please listen, follow directions, and participate.

Give each student a peanut and tell students to get acquainted with their peanuts. Allow two or three minutes for them to feel, look at, smell, shake, and squeeze their peanuts.

Have students place all of the peanuts on a table and tell them to turn their backs while you rearrange the peanuts. Then have students locate their own peanuts and take them back to their seats.

Ask the following questions:

1. Were you able to identify your peanut? Please explain.

2. In what ways is your peanut like the other peanuts?

3. In what ways is your peanut different from the other peanuts?

Then say, "Just as peanuts are both alike and different, so are people. We are going to discuss ways that people are alike and different."

Ask students to list ways people are alike and different. You may ask the students to make up a fantasy story based on the list of likes and differences that are generated.

Materials:

Peanuts in the shell

© 2003
www.allsucceed.com

- Other Awareness -

GATHER ALL THE FACTS

Purpose: Help students to learn and acknowledge the needs of others and to behave accordingly.

Tell the students:

> It is important that we are aware of the needs of others. This activity helps us learn more about their needs. Please listen, follow directions, and participate.

Discuss with the class how one could judge behavior only after all available information has been obtained.

Role-play for the class a situation in which a mistake is made and illustrate how behavior is sometimes judged or labeled before all information about the situation has been studied.

Discuss with the class mistakes that are inadvertently made when:

1. going to the lockers
2. responding in class
3. playing at recess or break
4. speaking with others
5. delivering messages

Ask students to determine ways of applying the activity ideas to other situations.

Notes:

Materials:

None

Notes:

- Other Awareness -

INDIVIDUAL DIFFERENCES

Purpose: Help students learn the uniqueness and differences of people.

Tell the students:

> It is important that we are aware of the uniqueness and differences of others so that we may feel happier and get along better. This activity helps us learn more about others. Please listen, follow directions, and participate.

Discuss with the group ways that people are individuals and, therefore, unique. This fact contributes to the well-being of other persons.

Discuss reasons that people differ in size, ability, and interests. Ask students to list ways that people benefit from those differences.

Ask students to relate this information to the impact on friendships and other relationships and situations.

Materials:

None

- Other Awareness -

THE JOY OF SHARING

Purpose: Help students learn to define and describe feelings related to personal experiences with others.

Tell the students:

> It is important that we know the way we feel about others and understand ways of explaining those feelings. This activity helps us learn ways of doing that. Please listen, follow directions, and participate.

Have the students discuss the happiness inherent in sharing.

Ask students to discuss the experience of giving gifts and the feeling they experience as the receiver opens their gift.

Ask each student to sketch two objects that he or she enjoys sharing with others. Then, in the group, ask the student to explain the sketches and the reasons he or she enjoys sharing the objects

Make a board display of the sketches or hang them in different areas of the room.

Ask students to determine ways to apply the ideas from the activity in other situations.

Notes:

Materials:

Drawing paper
Drawing supplies

Notes:

- Other Awareness -

COMPLEMENT EXPERIENCE

Purpose: Help students learn to define and describe feelings related to personal experiences with others.

Tell the students:

> It is important that we know the way we feel about others and understand ways of explaining those feelings. This activity helps us learn ways of doing that. Please listen, follow directions, and participate.

Discuss with the students the meaning of the word *complement*. Include the idea that, what one person lacks, another person has.

Divide the students into small groups. Divide one puzzle between groups. Ask the students in each group to complete their part of the puzzle.

The students will soon understand that the pieces they hold complement the pieces the rest of the groups have, just as one characteristic complements the other in people.

Ask students the way these ideas relate to other situations.

Materials:

Jigsaw puzzle

- Other Awareness -

GROWTH RATE DIFFERENCES

Purpose: Help students learn the uniqueness and differences of people.

Tell the students:

> It is important that we are aware of the uniqueness and differences of others so that we may feel happier and get along better. This activity helps us learn more about others. Please listen, follow directions, and participate.

Explain that just as all students do not grow at the same rate, neither do they learn at the same rate or react emotionally the same way.

Have the students draw pictures of other students, show the pictures to the group, and tell how students physically grow at different rates.

Discuss examples of mental growth. List math problems and vocabulary words that were unknown at the beginning of the school year that most students have mastered now, but at different rates.

Give examples of emotional growth. Ask students to discuss how they are not afraid of things they may have feared when they were younger.

Discuss the feelings that some may experience if others grow faster than they do in some ways. List different things that students can do if they feel concern. Also, ask students to determine things they can do to help others that may be having a concern.

Encourage others to talk to someone when they have questions about their growth. It is important to discuss that we are important, regardless of our growth process.

Notes:

Materials:

None

Notes:

- Other Awareness -

MAGIC WAND

Purpose: Help students learn the uniqueness and differences of people.

Tell the students:

> It is important that we are aware of the uniqueness and differences of others so that we may feel happier and get along better. This activity helps us learn more about others. Please listen, follow directions, and participate.

Read the following poem to the class:

MAGIC WAND

> Your magic wand can help you see
> Unique things about you and me.
> No one else writes or thinks the same—
> Our special magic is much more than our name.
> All the things we think, say, and do
> Become the magic that makes you, you.
> —T. R. Radd

Ask each student to write his or her name on a line. Ask three others to write that same name on three other lines. Do they all write the name the same?

Ask the students to take turns. Think a thought about something and ask others to guess what the thought is. Can they?

Discuss how even identical twins may be different in how they act, think, and so on.

Materials:
Writing paper
Pencils

© 2003
www.allsucceed.com

82

- Other Awareness -

THE IMPACT OF OUR NEEDS

Purpose: Help students learn to define and describe feelings related to personal experiences with others.

Tell the students:

> It is important that we know the way we feel about others and understand ways of explaining those feelings. This activity helps us learn ways of doing that. Please listen, follow directions, and participate.

Have a group discussion about how needs and feelings make us alike.

Students or the group leader lists on the board all of the needs they have in common. Discuss that, even though each is a unique person, there are some things that we all need and some feelings that we all choose to have.

Discuss with the students that needs and feelings are some of the reasons that we behave as we do.

List all of the needs that the students suggest into categories—physiological, safety, love, self-worth, and self-actualization. It might be best to call the first need *physical*. Most of the needs that the students come up with will probably be physical ones, so help them discover the safety, love, and self-worth needs.

Ask students about the relationship between their needs, feelings, and behavior. Discuss with students that when we can understand our needs and feelings better, we understand ways to make helpful behavior choices.

Notes:

Materials:

None

Notes:

- Other Awareness -

ALIKE OR DIFFERENT?

Purpose: Help students learn the uniqueness and differences of people.

Tell the students:

It is important that we are aware of the uniqueness and differences of others so that we may feel happier and get along better. This activity helps us learn more about others. Please listen, follow directions, and participate.

Remind students of the many ways in which people are alike and different by reviewing some of the students' ideas listed in earlier lessons. Discuss these questions:

1. Can you think of some times when you want to be like someone else?
2. Can you think of some times when you want to be different from someone else?
3. What are some of the reasons for wanting to be different from someone else?
4. What are some of the reasons for wanting to be like someone else?
5. What are some ways you are similar to other students in this classroom or group?
6. What are ways you differ from other students in this classroom or group?
7. What would our group be like if every student in it were exactly alike?
8. What would our group be like if every student in it were completely different?

Ask students to apply the activity information to other situations.

Materials:
None

www.allsucceed.com

- Other Awareness -

YOUR POINT OF VIEW?

Purpose: Help students learn the uniqueness and differences of people.

Tell the students:

> It is important that we are aware of the uniqueness and differences of others so that we may feel happier and get along better. This activity helps us learn more about others. Please listen, follow directions, and participate.

Discuss with the group how people view situations differently because each one sees a situation from his or her own point of view or frame of reference.

Ask for a volunteer to tell the group which game he or she best likes to play and explain the reasons. Then ask a fellow student who disagrees to explain which game he or she likes best to play and the reasons.

Ask for volunteers to tell the group the reasons they think the students liked different games.

Notes:

Materials:
None

Notes:

- Other Awareness -

YOUR ORIGINAL PRINT

Purpose: Help students learn the uniqueness and differences of people.

Duplicate and distribute the Your Original Print activity sheet. Discuss the following with the class:

> Every person has different marks on each finger. These marks are called fingerprints. Every fingerprint is different.

Have them look at their thumbs and fingers and see if they can detect the tiny lines. Have the students put their thumbprints in the proper place on their activity sheet. Discuss the value of thumbprints. Ask the students what they learned from this activity. Did they enjoy it? Provide an ink pad for printing their thumbprint.

Name: _____

Date: _____

My right thumbprint:

Ask students to draw or express ideas and feelings in the Creative Corner.

Materials:

Ink pad
Activity sheet

© 2003
www.allsucceed.com

86

- Activity sheet -

Your Original Print

Name: _____

Date: _____

My right thumbprint:

Draw or express your ideas and feelings in the Creative Corner.

```
C r e a t i v e
o
r
n
e
r
```

87

Notes:

- Other Awareness -

INTERVIEW EXPERIENCE

Purpose: Help students learn the uniqueness and differences of people.

Duplicate and distribute the Interview Experience activity sheet. Explain that the questions listed on the activity sheet are some things they might like to know about each other. Students think of other questions students might also want to ask and add those questions to their activity sheet.

Select three or four volunteers to be panel members and three or four to be interviewees for the following day.

Each day, before the activity begins, ask the student panel members to decide on the questions they wish to ask. It is important that the group leader clear all questions. Before the interview begins, assure the students that they have the right to refuse to answer any questions by saying, "I pass." Then have the panel members and interviewee introduce themselves and proceed with the interview.

    Questions are as follows:

1. Where were you born?
2. How many different places have you lived?
3. How many brothers and sisters do you have?
4. What are their names and ages?
5. Do you have a pet?
6. What is your favorite holiday? Please explain.
7. What is your favorite food?
8. (Other)

After the student information is shared, ask students to state things they learned about other students in their group. Ask students to include similarities they discovered among student interviewers.

Materials:

Activity sheet

- Activity sheet -

Interview Experience

1. Where were you born?

2. How many different places have you lived?

3. How many brothers and sisters do you have?

4. What are their names and ages?

5. Do you have a pet?

6. What is your favorite holiday? Please explain.

7. What is your favorite food?

8. (Other)

Notes:

- Other Awareness -

ALL VIEWPOINTS

Purpose: Help students to learn and acknowledge the views of others and to behave accordingly.

Tell the students:

> It is important that we are aware of the views of others. This activity helps us learn more about their needs. Please listen, follow directions, and participate.

This activity supports the concept of looking at things from all viewpoints and can be used at any time during the year when it seems appropriate. The song, *Walk a Mile in My Shoes*, recorded by Joe South, might be used as an introduction to this activity.

Play the song and ask students to discuss its meaning. Then the group might agree, that at any time one student feels that another is acting in a "one-sided" manner, he may immediately give the other side.

This could be a discussion between the two students only, or the whole group might participate. It is not necessary to reach a definite conclusion. The important thing is that the students begin to think of others' views and other ways to look at things.

Materials:

Song: *Walk A Mile In My Shoes*

90

Notes:

- Other Awareness -

BASIC SIMILARITIES

Purpose: Help students learn the uniqueness and differences of people.

Tell the students:

> It is important that we are aware of the uniqueness and differences of others so that we may feel happier and get along better. This activity helps us learn more about others. Please listen, follow directions, and participate.

Ask students to draw a ball and decorate it with different colors. Then show the pictures and discuss with the students that they are all balls, even though they may be different in appearance.

This illustrates that things can be basically the same but have different characteristics.

Discuss the way individual differences relates to this experience.

Materials:

Drawing paper
Drawing supplies

Notes:

- Other Awareness -

ANIMAL INSTRUCTION

Purpose: Help students learn the uniqueness and differences of animals.

Tell the students:

It is important that we are aware of the uniqueness and differences of animals. This activity helps us learn more about their needs. Please listen, follow directions, and participate.

Another dimension to learning is animal learning. Ask the students if they have ever wanted their pets or an animal to learn something (e.g., a trick, to use a scratching post, or to not jump on the table).

Students who have taught their animal a particular thing or have watched animals learn a trick might be asked how they did it and how well the animal learned. Students might wonder whether there were any problems, what caused them, and how they were resolved.

After the discussion, suggest that students teach something to animals kept at school, perhaps in a learning center.

The results of teaching more than one animal could provide a basis for discussion about rates of learning or individual differences.

The students may prefer to teach their own pets something. Select volunteers from those students who want to teach their pets at home.

The group could design a plan for the individual student to teach his or her animal something, and he or she could report back to the group the results of their plan and any problems that have occurred.

Materials:

Animal pets at school or at home

Notes:

- Other Awareness -

YOUR TALENTS AND ABILITIES

Purpose: Help students learn the uniqueness and differences of people.

Tell the students:

> It is important that we are aware of the uniqueness and differences of others so that we may feel happier and get along better. This activity helps us learn more about others. Please listen, follow directions, and participate.

Ask the students to bring pictures illustrating differences in talents and abilities. Discuss ways that each student can make his own unique and worthwhile contribution in such areas as team sports, games, classwork, music, and others.

Discuss the following questions:

1. What would happen if everyone were exactly alike?

2. What are some things that can be done best by people who are short, tall, fast, slow, etc.

3. Explain the reasons people have different talents and abilities.

Discuss the benefits we all receive due to our differences.

Ask students to role-play different talents of the group.

Materials:

Pictures from various sources: resource books the Internet, or magazines

93

Notes:

- Other Awareness -

WAYS WE DIFFER

Purpose: Help students learn the uniqueness and differences of people.

Tell the students:

> It is important that we are aware of the uniqueness and differences of others so that we may feel happier and get along better. This activity helps us learn more about others. Please listen, follow directions, and participate.

Write the following statement on the board:

> In our room, some students are _____
> _____.

Ask the students to name ways they differ from one another. For example, some students are quiet, some are loud, some are tall, some short, some friendly, some shy, and so on. List all contributions on the board.

Then say:

> In looking at the list we have developed, we can see that we have many individual differences in our group.
>
> 1. Do any of these differences require special consideration from the rest of the class? Please explain.
>
> 2. What are some of the things we do for people who are different? Give the reasons we do these things?

Materials:

None

Discuss the information and relate it to ways of using everyone's talents, supporting student challenges and helping everyone know they are valued in the group.

Notes:

- Other Awareness -

WHO IS IT? GAME

Purpose: Help students learn the uniqueness and differences of people and the way their personality traits are seen by others.

Tell the students:

> It is important that we are aware of the uniqueness and differences of others so that we may feel happier and get along better. This activity helps us learn more about others. Please listen, follow directions, and participate.

Ask five students to stand in front with their backs to the class. Select one student to be "it" by writing a name on paper and holding it up for the group to see.

Ask all five to turn around and face the group. The group gives clues—descriptions, characteristics, and so on. After five clues are given, the five students discuss which one of them is it and name the person.

If the first guess is correct, they receive five points. If not, continue with four clues, then three clues, and so on, following the procedure until the "it" person on the team is guessed.

Follow this procedure with each team. The team with the highest number of points is the winner.

If the activity is repeated, select different students to be on the teams.

Materials:

None

Notes:

- Other Awareness -

IDENTIFICATION GAME

Purpose: Help students learn the uniqueness and differences of people and help them see themselves as others see them.

Tell the students:

> It is important that we are aware of the uniqueness and differences of others and how others see us. This activity helps us learn more about others. Please listen, follow directions, and participate.

Select one student to be a police officer and another to be a parent. The parent asks, "Police officer, can you help me find my lost child?"

The parent then proceeds to describe one of the students in the group. When the student is found and identified, the parent becomes the police officer and the missing child becomes the parent, and the game is repeated.

Materials:

None

© 2003
www.allsucceed.com

Notes:

- Other Awareness -

PHRASES THAT DESCRIBE

Purpose: Help students learn the uniqueness and differences of people.

Tell the students:

> It is important that we are aware of the uniqueness and differences of others so that we may feel happier and get along better. This activity helps us learn more about others. Please listen, follow directions, and participate.

Collect magazine pictures of people of different ages, races, and sexes. Ask students to bring additional pictures to add to those available.

For each picture, ask the students to write or vocalize a simple descriptive phrase.

Discuss the differences and changes that students notice in their descriptions between the groups and within the groups.

Ask students to write a short story using the simple descriptive phrases they have said or written.

Materials:

Magazines
Photos
Pictures from
 various sources,
 such as Internet

Notes:

- Other Awareness -

DECISION PUZZLE

Purpose: Help students learn the uniqueness and differences of people.

Tell the students:

It is important that we are aware of the uniqueness and differences of others so that we may feel happier and get along better. This activity helps us learn more about others. Please listen, follow directions, and participate.

Read the following to the class:

One morning, Bill brought a new book to school. He had bought it with his own money. It was all about cars and had very exciting pictures in it. At break, he left it in his desk; but when he returned, it was gone. As he started out to find his teacher in the hall, he happened to notice the expression on Tom's face. He knew Tom had it. And Tom didn't deny it. Instead, he just dared Bill to get it back. Before the others knew what happened, the two were rolling all over the floor. No one knew what to do and they were relieved when Mr. Taylor hurried in to separate the fighters.

When things were quiet again, Mr. Taylor asked, "Bill, what happened?"

Bill explained about the book. Mr. Taylor turned to Tom. "Did you?"

"Yes," admitted Tom.

"Why?" asked Mr. Taylor.

"I don't know," said Tom.

List the clues from the story that we can use to solve this puzzle.

This activity may continue with the Decision Puzzle Clues activity on the next page.

Materials:
None

98

Notes:

- Other Awareness -

DECISION PUZZLE CLUES

Purpose: Help students learn the uniqueness and differences of people.

Tell the students:

It is important that we are aware of the uniqueness and differences of others so that we may feel happier and get along better. This activity helps us learn more about others. Please listen, follow directions, and participate.

Read the story in the Decision Puzzle activity on the previous page. Ask students to list the possible clues and determine the clues that can help solve the puzzle. Ask the students to decide if the clue is helpful in understanding Tom's behavior. Compare the clue list selected with the list of clues generated during the Decision Puzzle activity.

1. Tom has blue eyes.
2. His mother works parttime.
3. Tom has a toothache.
4. He had cookies for breakfast.
5. He has an older sister.
6. He is going to visit his grandparents tomorrow.
7. Sometimes he teases younger kids.
8. His hands were dirty.
9. His mother took his sister shopping Saturday.
10. His best friend has a new baseball mitt.
11. The others on his team always choose him to pitch.
12. Sometimes he is tardy for school.
13. He often runs errands for a neighbor.
14. His dad brought home a new bike for his sister.
15. He wants to deliver papers, but his mom thinks he's too young.
16. In the first grade, he was very shy and quiet.
17. He collects bugs, but his mom doesn't like them.
18. Tom has no books of his own.
19. Tom is 10 years old. (Add clues if necessary.)

Discuss ways the story applies to situations with students.

Materials:

Clues generated during decision puzzle activity

Notes:

- Other Awareness -

WHAT IS HAPPINESS?

Purpose: Help students learn to define and describe feelings related to personal career choices.

Duplicate and distribute the What Is Happiness? activity sheet. This activity compares people's ideas of happiness through a discussion of various career persons. Above the career title in each box, students can draw pictures to illustrate what happiness is to each. Discuss whether or not all persons on the chart would agree on what happiness is. Discuss similarities as well as differences.

Example:

Pet store owner	Business person	Student
Hunter	Farmer	Teacher
Author	Photographer	Mechanic

Materials:
Activity sheet

www.allsucceed.com

- Activity sheet -

What Is Happiness?

Above the career title in each box, draw pictures to illustrate what happiness is to each.

Pet store owner	Business person	Student
Hunter	Farmer	Teacher
Author	Photographer	Mechanic

Notes:

- Other Awareness -

STUDENT FOR THE DAY

Purpose: Help students learn the uniqueness and differences of people.

Tell the students:

> It is important that we are aware of the uniqueness and differences of others so that we may feel happier and get along better. This activity helps us learn more about others. Please listen, follow directions, and participate.

Choose one student to be student for the day. Ask the remaining students to describe all the things that this student does well (e.g., sings loud and clear, catches fly balls, is polite, is helpful, is an accurate reader, etc.). Join in this activity also and state additional comments about the student.

Encourage students to be sincere in their comments; that is, to comment on points that they have observed or experienced in their relationship with their fellow students.

After several persons have commented on the student's positive characteristics, have the student thank the group for their interest and then tell something he or she wants to improve and is working on at this time.

Do the activity once a week until all have had a turn.

Materials:
None

Notes:

- Other Awareness -

TRAITS OF BEING FRIENDLY

Purpose: Help students to learn and acknowledge the needs of others and to behave accordingly.

Tell the students:

> It is important that we are aware of the needs of others. This activity helps us learn more about their needs. Please listen, follow directions, and participate.

Discuss with the group the need of human beings to be social and have relationships with peers. A key to harmonious human relationships is to treat others as you would like to be treated. Elicit from the students traits of a friendly person and list on them on the board.

For example:

kindness

thoughtfulness

acceptance of differences

being fun to work and play with

working and playing well in groups

sharing with others, and so on

Have the students copy the list and make a checklist.

Have them check off their own behavior of friendliness toward others and give personal examples.

Ask students to select one thing on the list to improve.

Materials:

None

Notes:

- Other Awareness -

HANDLING WINNING DESIRES

Purpose: Help students learn to define and describe feelings related to personal experiences with others.

Tell the students:

> It is important that we know the way we feel about others and understand ways of explaining those feelings. This activity helps us learn ways of doing that. Please listen, follow directions, and participate.

The desire to win may foster feelings that can cause a person to hurt another. Ask the class to name some situations in their environment in which someone wins and someone loses. List their responses on the board.

The students may feel that many of their daily experiences are competitive. Some students, as well as adults, feel that in almost everything they do, they will either win or lose.

Ask:

1. How do you feel when you want to do well but you think others will do better?

2. How can you express yourself without competing with someone?

3. When you lose, how could you act?

4. Do you ever act differently than you feel?

Have a class discussion after each question has been answered by several students.

Materials:
None

- Other Awareness -

ANGER AND BEHAVIOR

Purpose: Help students learn to define and describe feelings related to personal experiences with others.

Tell the students:

> It is important that we know the way we feel about others and understand ways of explaining those feelings. This activity helps us learn ways of doing that. Please listen, follow directions, and participate.

Ask the students to write some of the things that they choose to feel angry about and what they do when they become angry.

Then in small discussion groups or as a total class, decide whether these methods are helpful or hurtful in terms of the long-range effects. Ask the students to suggest helpful ways of behaving in the situation.

Be sure that students discuss these feelings in an understanding manner. The main goal is to develop constructive or helpful methods of handling angry feelings.

Notes:

Materials:

None

Notes:

- Other Awareness -

CHARADES

Purpose: Help students learn ways messages in communication are sent nonverbally.

Duplicate and cut into sections the Charades activity sheet. You may add a few additional messages in the blank boxes on the activity sheet. Before the lesson begins, place the charade messages listed on the activity sheet in a box. Divide the class into two teams. Tell them they are going to play charades.

Have each team count off. The number one player on the first team is to take a message out of the box, study it briefly, give it to the group leader, and then work to communicate the message to his or her team without speaking. Tell members of the opposite team to remain silent. Each player will be allowed one minute. If the player's team has not guessed the message, the other team has one minute to do it. Score one point for the team that guesses correctly.

Next, the number one player from the second team does the same and the procedure is repeated. The first team to reach seven points wins.

Messages:

I like you.	I am so ashamed.
Will you help me?	I am scared.
I am sad.	I will not give up.
We won!	I am proud.
I am furious.	I don't want to do it.
I am bored.	What a surprise!

Materials:

Activity sheet

© 2003
www.allsucceed.com

106

- Activity sheet -

Charades

Charade messages:

I like you.	I am so ashamed.
Will you help me?	I am scared.
I am sad.	I will not give up.
We won!	I am proud.
I am furious.	I don't want to do it.
I am bored.	What a surprise!

Notes:

- Other Awareness -

POSTURE EXPRESSION

Purpose: Help students learn to define and describe feelings related to personal experiences with others.

Tell the students:

> It is important that we know the way we feel about others and understand ways of explaining those feelings. This activity helps us learn ways of doing that. Please listen, follow directions, and participate.

Give each student three pipe cleaners. Tell students that they are to make a pipe-cleaner person that is expressing a feeling through its posture.

When students have completed the task, ask for volunteers to show their pipe-cleaner person to the group, one at a time. Have them give a brief description of how their person is feeling and relate an incident when they felt this way.

Display the pipe-cleaner people at some convenient place.

Materials:

Pipe cleaners

Notes:

- Other Awareness -

IMPACT OF ENVIRONMENT

Purpose: Help students learn to define and describe feelings related to personal experiences with others.

Tell the students:

> It is important that we know the way we feel about others and understand ways of explaining those feelings. This activity helps us learn ways of doing that. Please listen, follow directions, and participate.

To show the effect surroundings have on feelings, ask each student to design a room (e.g., a sad room, peaceful room, etc.). Special emphasis could be given not only to the obvious color elements in the room, but also to space, shapes, textures, types of furniture, views and things that might affect the mood of the room's occupant.

In addition, the students might select from newspapers, magazines, or whatever sources are available to them that would fit an assigned concept. The drawings and pictures could be compared by the class to see which elements of design affect many people the same way and which designs have a varying impact with individuals.

It might also be interesting for the students to create environments that would lead to more subjective interpretations, such as a proud garden, a jealous park, or a guilty store.

Materials:

Drawing paper
Drawing supplies
Optional:
　Newspaper
　Internet

© 2003
www.allsucceed.com

Notes:

- Other Awareness -

TALKING DIFFERENCES

Purpose: Help students learn and describe feelings related to talking.

Duplicate and distribute the Talking Differences activity sheet which describes different kinds of talkers. Complete the activity sheet, then discuss responses with the group.

Question: What time is it?
Little Talker: About 2:30.
Medium Talker: I don't have a watch, but I think it's about 2:30.
Big Talker: For the first time in a long time, I didn't wear my watch today. I left it on the breakfast table, right by the toaster, I think. But I happen to look at a clock about 30 minutes ago.

1. Can you think of one person who is usually a little talker?

   _____

   medium talker? _____

   big talker? _____

2. For each different situation, write the kind of talker that you are most likely to be: little, medium, or big.

   1. With a small group of friends._____

   2. With adults you do not know well._____

   3. In a large party. _____

   4. Caught doing something that is hurtful. _____

Materials:

Activity sheet

© 2003
www.allsucceed.com

110

- Activity sheet -

Talking Differences

There are all kinds of talkers.

Question: What time is it?
Little Talker: About 2:30.
Medium Talker: I don't have a watch, but I think it's about 2:30.
Big Talker: For the first time in a long time, I didn't wear my watch today. I left it on the breakfast table, right by the toaster, I think. But I happen to look at a clock about 30 minutes ago.

1. Can you think of one person who is usually a little talker? _____

   medium talker? _____

   big talker? _____

2. For each different situation, write the kind of talker that you are most likely to be: little, medium, or big.

   1. With a small group of friends. _____

   2. With adults you do not know well. _____

   3. In a large party. _____

   4. Caught doing something that is hurtful. _____

Notes:

- Other Awareness -

ATTITUDE FACTORS

Purpose: Help students learn the uniqueness and differences of people.

Tell the students:

It is important that we are aware of the uniqueness and differences of others so that we may feel happier and get along better. This activity helps us learn more about others. Please listen, follow directions, and participate.

Ask the group to assemble photos or magazine pictures of people of various sizes, races, weights, and so on. As the students look at the pictures, ask such questions as the following:

1. Which of these people would not be helpful to others as a peace corps worker, a doctor, a teacher, a police officer, or a dentist?

2. Which of these people would not make a contribution to all people by composing a song, writing an exciting story, or painting a picture?

3. Which of these people would not be your friend, your minister or rabbi, or your neighbor?

(The conclusion would be that individual differences in size, weight, race, sex, or color would not be factors in determining one's attitude toward others.)

Later, students can discuss contributions to society that can be or have been made by all types of individuals.

Materials:

Photos
Magazine pictures
Pictures from
  various sources

© 2003
www.allsucceed.com

- Other Awareness -

DIFFERENCES OF OPINION

Purpose: Help students learn the uniqueness and differences of people.

Tell the students:

>It is important that we are aware of the uniqueness and differences of others so that we may feel happier and get along better. This activity helps us learn ways to know. Please listen, follow directions, and participate.

Help students to see the different ideas and values they have from others. Have each student draw a picture of the most beautiful, the funniest, or the most frightening thing that he or she has ever seen.

Have everyone draw about the same theme. Have students tell about their pictures. Point out that we are often different in what each of us considers beautiful, funny, and so on.

Notes:

Materials:

Drawing paper
Drawing supplies

Notes:

- Other Awareness -

WHAT'S THE FEELING?

Purpose: Help students learn to define and describe gestures related to communicating feelings to others.

Tell the students:

> It is important that we know the way we feel about others and understand ways of explaining those feelings. This activity helps us learn ways of doing that. Please listen, follow directions, and participate.

Ask for student volunteers to each select a feeling from the appropriate Feeling Words Lists activity sheet found beginning on page 293. Ask each volunteer to whisper the gesture to you before demonstrating it. Have the student stand in front and imitate the gesture so that all feeling communication is done nonverbally through gestures.

Ask the other students to guess what feeling the gesture communicates. Repeat this procedure with other students using other feeling gestures chosen at random from the activity sheet or from a different source. Then ask students if they can recall other gestures discussed during previous activity experiences. Ask for volunteers to demonstrate those gestures and feelings. Have the other students guess the feeling that is being communicated.

Ask students how the impact of others understanding their communication messages may have on their relationships with others.

Discuss ways of applying the ideas generated to other life situations.

Materials:

Activity sheet
Feeling Words
Lists

- Other Awareness -

GESTURE DEMONSTRATIONS

Purpose: Help students learn to define and describe gestures related to personal experiences with others.

Tell the students:

It is important that we know the way we feel about others and understand ways of explaining those feelings. This activity helps us learn ways of doing that. Please listen, follow directions, and participate.

Ask students if anyone can tell the group what the word *gesture* means. (The use of motions or our body or limbs to express a meaning.) Then demonstrate the 10 examples below, one at a time. After each one, ask, "What does this gesture mean?"

1. Hand waving (Hello)
2. Arm extended forward, palm forward (Stop!)
3. Finger over lips (Asking for quiet)
4. Cupping an ear (Can't hear)
5. Upturning palms (To receive something)
6. Thumbs down (No!)
7. Thumbs up (Okay or yes!)
8. Thumb and index finger forming a circle (Okay sign)
9. Crooking forefinger (Come!)
10. Fingers crossed (Good luck!)

After all gestures have been shown, divide the class into four groups. Ask each group to create a role-play using as many of the gestures as possible.

Notes:

Materials:

None

Notes:

- Other Awareness -

SHARING FUN

Purpose: Help students to learn and acknowledge the needs of others and to behave accordingly.

Tell the students:

It is important that we are aware of the needs of others. This activity helps us learn more about their needs. Please listen, follow directions, and participate.

Ask students to discuss ways that sharing with someone can be of mutual benefit.

Ask the students to make a list of things (both tangible and intangible) that can be more valuable or enjoyable when shared (e.g., picnics, games, memories, jokes, etc.).

Discuss the concept with the group. Ask the students to give examples. The students may want to role-play examples with a partner or small group.

Materials:
None

116

- Other Awareness -

ENJOYMENT OF SHARING

Purpose: Help students learn to define and describe feelings related to personal experiences with others.

Tell the students:

> It is important that we know the way we feel about others and understand ways of explaining those feelings. This activity helps us learn ways of doing that. Please listen, follow directions, and participate.

Discuss with the students how many things they have that can be shared and how sharing can enhance the enjoyment of one's possessions.

Ask the students to draw pictures of things they have enjoyed sharing with someone else. Display and discuss the pictures.

Ask students to determine ways to apply activity ideas to other situations.

Notes:

Materials:
Drawing paper
Drawing supplies

© 2003
www.allsucceed.com

Notes:

- Other Awareness -

STORY FEELINGS FACES

Purpose: Help students learn to define and describe feelings related to personal experiences with others.

Tell the students:

> It is important that we know the way we feel about others and understand ways of explaining those feelings. This activity helps us learn ways of doing that. Please listen, follow directions, and participate.

Discuss with the students that the feelings communicated in facial expressions are related to various causes.

Ask students to find pictures of faces which communicate feelings in newspapers or magazines. Help them read and understand the accompanying stories that go with the pictures.

Invite them to read or retell the stories to the rest of the class. Ask the students to determine if the picture matches the story ideas.

Discuss the stories and feelings with the class.

Materials:

Newspaper and magazine pictures and stories

- Other Awareness -

FEELINGS ROLE-PLAY

Purpose: Help students learn to define and describe feelings related to personal experiences with others.

Tell the students:

> It is important that we know the way we feel about others and understand ways of explaining those feelings. This activity helps us learn ways of doing that. Please listen, follow directions, and participate.

Divide the students into four groups. Ask each group to compose a short role-play about a school situation involving several different feelings. Urge them to exaggerate the facial expressions that go with the words and actions in their role-play.

When all groups are ready, have each one present its role-play. After each role-play, allow time for the student audience to identify the feelings expressed.

Encourage all student efforts.

Optional: You may suggest that students make paper masks to help exaggerate their presentations.

Notes:

Materials:
Optional:
　Paper
　Scissors
　Art supplies

Notes:

- Other Awareness -

CARTOON CREATION

Purpose: Help students learn to define and describe feelings related to personal experiences with others.

Tell the students:

It is important that we know the way we feel about others and understand ways of explaining those feelings. This activity helps us learn ways of doing that. Please listen, follow directions, and participate.

Ask the students to draw a sequence of behaviors by creating a cartoon strip. The activity can be developed as you discuss each aspect of anger. Each student divides a sheet of paper into three frames, either by folding or by drawing lines.

Steps:

1. In frame two, the students can draw a picture of an angry person.

2. After discussing causes of anger, they can draw the situation in frame one that might have caused the person in frame two to become angry.

3. After discussing the effects of anger, they can draw in frame three some of the possible effects of the frame two person's anger.

Discussion questions:

1. Is the angry person hurting anyone? How else might he or she act?

2. How might you feel if you were this angry person?

3. How might you act if you were him or her?

Materials:
Drawing paper
Drawing supplies

- Other Awareness -

COLORS AND FEELINGS

Purpose: Help students learn to define and describe feelings related to personal experiences with others.

Tell the students:

> It is important that we know the way we feel about others and understand ways of explaining those feelings. This activity helps us learn ways of doing that. Please listen, follow directions, and participate.

Discuss with the students that when we want to describe how a person is feeling, we sometimes use the name of a color. For example, we might say, "Jim is in a blue mood" because he is moping around or sad; or "Tom is in the pink," meaning he's feeling really good.

Ask students to form groups of four to six and ask each group to elect a recorder. Ask them to think of all the expressions that link feelings and colors and then to list them.

Have recorders read the lists. Respond to each item and make sure the reasons for color/feeling combinations have been made clear by the group.

Accept original responses and familiar ones. Collect the lists. After eliminating repetitions, write a master list of expressions on the board.

Allow ample time to discuss the list. Groups may write a story incorporating as many feeling and descriptions that they can use.

Notes:

Materials:

None

Notes:

- Other Awareness -

EMPATHY FOR OTHERS

Purpose: Help students learn to define and describe encouragement related to personal experiences with others.

Tell the students:

> It is important that we know the way we can encourage others and understand ways encouragement is helpful. This activity helps us learn ways of doing that. Please listen, follow directions, and participate.

Discuss with the students the importance of empathizing with people in difficulty and how to express encouragement.

List the following or similar incidents on the board and ask the students to draw a picture about one situation and to write a caption telling what to do or say to the person in the situation that may help him or her choose to feel better.

1. A girl or woman has just finished painting a picture and spills paint all over it.
2. A boy or man had a part in a play and forgot his lines while everybody was watching.
3. A friend missed a fly ball in the outfield during an important game.
4. Your friend was scolded or put down in front of the class.
5. One of your friends was not invited to another friend's party.
6. A student in your class is being bothered by a bully.
7. Your mother has had a very difficult day and the baby is crying for attention.
8. Your parents feel bad because they cannot buy something you want.

Materials:
None

© 2003
www.allsucceed.com

Notes:

- Other Awareness -

HELPING OTHERS

Purpose: Help students to learn and acknowledge the needs of others and to behave accordingly.

Tell the students:

> It is important that we are aware of the needs of others. This activity helps us learn more about their needs. Please listen, follow directions, and participate.

Help students appreciate the feelings that human beings hold in common.

Discuss the meaning to the thought, "It can't be better for me unless it's better for you."

Have the students search through newspapers to find examples of current events that cause people either happiness or unhappiness.

Ask students to brainstorm ways of helping each other in both happy and unhappy situations.

Discuss the examples and relate the information to improvements for home and school.

Materials:

Newspapers

Notes:

- Other Awareness -

HONESTY EXPERIENCE

Purpose: Help students to learn and acknowledge the needs of others and to behave accordingly.

Tell the students:

It is important that we are aware of the needs of others. This activity helps us learn more about their needs. Please listen, follow directions, and participate.

Pass out a list of words that the students probably would not know. Ask each student to get up and define one of the words. The students are to convince the others that they know the definition and then use the word in a sentence.

After each definition, the group decides whether the student knew the definition–which is possible–or faked it.

After one student has finished and the group has decided and discussed the reason they decided the way they did, tell the students the real definition. After all the students have taken a turn, the group can discuss persuasion and honesty, giving reasons they believed some students, and explaining the reasons they didn't believe others. Is what seems honest always honest? Is there any way you can tell if someone is being honest?

Ask students to determine ways to use the information from this activity.

Materials:

Words
Definitions

Notes:

- Other Awareness -

HANDLING ANGER

Purpose: Help students learn to define and describe feelings related to personal experiences with others.

Tell the students:

> It is important that we know the way we feel about others and understand ways of explaining those feelings. This activity helps us learn ways of doing that. Please listen, follow directions, and participate.

Divide students into small groups and ask them to share times when they got angry.

Ask students to make a list of experiences in which they have felt angry or frustrated. After they have completed the list, have them discuss helpful and hurtful ways of handling these feelings.

Ask the small groups to summarize the small group ideas and share them with the group.

Ask each student to select one helpful way of handling these feeling and then to test their plan. Ask students to observe each other and to report progress.

Materials:
None

Notes:

- Other Awareness -

TEACHER COMMUNICATION

Purpose: Help students learn the uniqueness and differences of people.

Tell the students:

> It is important that we are aware of the uniqueness and differences of others so that we may feel happier and get along better. This activity helps us learn more about others. Please listen, follow directions, and participate.

Have the students draw a picture of a teacher (or other person, such as a counselor) and then explain it in terms of

1. what he or she is doing

2. what other things the teacher (or other person) does.

3. how they feel about the teacher (or other person).

4. how they think the teacher (or other person) feels about them.

Ask the students what they think a person has to do to become a teacher (or other person, such as a counselor). This may be an opportunity for you to share part of yourself as a person by talking about your background.

During sharing time, you may offer pictures of your family, activities you enjoy, favorite hobbies, and so on. Encourage the students' questions. It may also be effective to allow students to play the role of their teacher, counselor, or other person.

Many teachers (or other persons) may not realize that, often, students do not regard them as real human beings with lives beyond their roles at school.

Materials:

Teacher or other information to share

- Other Awareness -

EXPRESSING FEARS

Purpose: Help students learn to define and describe feelings related to personal experiences with others.

Tell the students:

> It is important that we know the way we feel about others and understand ways of explaining those feelings. This activity helps us learn ways of doing that. Please listen, follow directions, and participate.

Discuss characters from well-known stories, such as *Little Red Riding Hood*, *Hansel and Gretel*, *The Three Billy Goats Gruff, The Three Little Pigs* in terms of:

1. what their fears are.

2. how they react to their fears.

3. how they might feel if exposed to a similar fear at another time.

Adapt the *Who's Afraid of the Big Bad Wolf?* song into one that tells the fears of the students in the class.

Optional: Ask students to draw a picture about their fear and a way they help themselves and others.

Notes:

Materials:

Songs and stories
Drawing paper
Drawing supplies

Notes:

- Other Awareness -

HANDLING CLASSROOM ANGER

Purpose: Help students learn to define and describe feelings related to personal experiences with others.

Tell the students:

> It is important that we know the way we feel about others and understand ways of explaining those feelings. This activity helps us learn ways of doing that. Please listen, follow directions, and participate.

This activity can be done in two parts.

Discuss the questions from the viewpoint of angry students and then from the viewpoint of an angry teacher. In this way, you will gain great insight into each other's feelings.

Questions for discussion:

1. What sometimes causes students to choose to be angry in the classroom?

2. What can they do about these things?

3. What usually happens when they get angry?

4. What kind of help can students find when they choose to feel angry?

5. How do they know when the teacher or student is angry?

6, How do they feel when the teacher or student is angry?

7. How do they act when the teacher or student is angry?

Ask students to determine ways of applying the ideas generated from this activity experience.

Materials:

None

© 2003
www.allsucceed.com

- Other Awareness -

BUILDING BRIDGES

Purpose: Help students learn to define and describe feelings related to personal experiences with others.

Tell the students:

It is important that we know the way we feel about others and understand ways of explaining those feelings. This activity helps us learn ways of doing that. Please listen, follow directions, and participate.

Read and discuss the following poem:

BUILDING BRIDGES

When things happen that rub me the wrong way
Those are the times I don't know what to say!
When my favorite cup fell and broke
You laughed and thought it was some kind of a joke.
When I finally found success on a test
You didn't notice I'd done my best,
And when I felt sad and wanted to cry
It puzzled me that you didn't know why.
Even though we are different as two people can be,
Can we still build a bridge between you and me?
—T. R. Radd

Related activities:

1. Review each statement and help the students label the emotion involved.

2. Pick out the words that are clues to emotions such as cry, joke, laughed, sad, puzzled, etc.

3. Have the student choose the part of the verse they like best.

Notes:

Materials:

Optional:
Feeling Words Lists beginning on page 293

Notes:

- Other Awareness -

DEFINE HURTFUL BEHAVIOR

Purpose: Help students to learn and acknowledge the needs of others and to behave accordingly.

Tell the students:

> It is important that we are aware of the needs of others. This activity helps us learn more about their needs. Please listen, follow directions, and participate.

Have the students bring in pictures of people who are hurting others.

Ask these questions after they have viewed them.

1. What is happening in this picture?

2. What can we call this picture?

3. How might these persons feel?

4. Explain the way these actions might hurt others?

Discuss the ways students can stay safe and help each other.

Materials:
Newspaper
  pictures
Magazine pictures
Other pictures

www.allsucceed.com

130

- Other Awareness -

SHARING EXPERIENCES

Purpose: Help students learn to define and describe feelings related to personal experiences with others.

Tell the students:

> It is important that we know the way we feel about others and understand ways of explaining those feelings. This activity helps us learn ways of doing that. Please listen, follow directions, and participate.

Discuss with the class group specific examples of the many things that can be shared, such as ideas, great times, memories, jokes, and games.

For several consecutive days, ask each student to record the number of times he or she has shared something with someone and how many times someone has shared with him or her.

Discuss student results and reactions.

Ask students to determine their feelings towards others when they were sharing with others or others were sharing with them.

Notes:

Materials:

Paper
Pencil

Notes:

- Other Awareness -

DIFFERENT REACTIONS

Purpose: Help students learn that different people react differently in situations.

Duplicate and distribute the Different Reactions activity sheet. Discuss with the group how people have different feelings toward the same situations. Give as an example some students playing baseball and breaking a window. Ask, "How would you feel if you were each of these people?"

Mark an X on the line showing how you would feel.

Batter

_____ "Gosh, I didn't think I could hit that far."

_____ "Oh no, now I'm really in trouble."

_____ "Ha! Ha! Look what I did."

Homeowner

_____ "Look at what those stupid kids did."

_____ "I knew this would happen sooner or later."

_____ "I'm going to call your parents."

Pitcher

_____ "I'm getting out of here."

_____ "I'll help you pay for it."

_____ "What a hit!"

Discuss the different feelings expressed.

Materials:

Activity sheet

- Activity sheet -

Different Reactions

Mark an X on the line showing how you would feel.

Batter
___ "Gosh, I didn't think I could hit that far."
___ "Oh no, now I'm really in trouble."
___ "Ha! Ha! Look what I did."

Homeowner
___ "Look at what those stupid kids did."
___ "I knew this would happen sooner or later."
___ "I'm going to call your parents."

Pitcher
___ "I'm getting out of here."
___ "I'll help you pay for it."
___ "What a hit!"

133

Grow with Guidance® © 2003
www.allsucceed.com

Notes:

- Other Awareness -

OWNER LOCATION GAME

Purpose: Help students learn the uniqueness and differences of people to determine strategies for relating to others.

Tell the students:

> It is important that we are aware of the uniqueness and differences of others so that we may feel happier and get along better. This activity helps us learn more about others. Please listen, follow directions, and participate.

Explain to the group that you are going to play a game called, Take Me To My Home.

Select one student to cover her eyes while someone from the group puts an article on the floor behind her.

The student discovers the article and takes it back to its owner. If she does not know the owner, she may ask questions to help her find the object's home.

Repeat the game until all students have an opportunity to participate.

Ask the students to determine ways they can apply what they learned about others in their group.

Materials:

Different student articles

Notes:

- Other Awareness -

POSTURE COMMUNICATION

Purpose: Help students learn the nonverbal communication of others.

Tell the students:

> It is important that we are aware of the uniqueness and differences of others so that we may feel happier and get along better. This activity helps us learn about ways to communicate feelings without talking.

Ask if anyone can tell the group what the word *posture* means (the position in which we hold our bodies). Model each of the postures described below and ask students to imitate it. While they are imitating the posture, ask:

1. What feeling or feelings do you think this posture communicates?

2. Have you ever felt like this? What was happening to cause you to choose to feel this way?

Postures:

1. Standing, head down, shoulders slumped.

2. Standing, head erect, shoulders back.

3. Standing, with feet spread, fists on hips.

4. Standing, with arms tucked in close to body, shoulders in, head down.

5. Sitting, slumped in chair, legs crossed.

6. Sitting on edge of chair, back straight, eyes up.

Materials:

None

Notes:

- Other Awareness -

A RADIANT GLOW

Purpose: Help students learn to define and describe feelings related to personal experiences with others.

Tell the students:

> It is important that we know the way we feel about others and understand ways of explaining those feelings. This activity helps us learn ways of doing that. Please listen, follow directions, and participate.

Read the following poem to the students. Discuss the meaning of the poem and explain difficult words. Use the questions supplied for discussion.

> One fine day I met a yellow bear
> Whose yellow hair left her in despair.
> Her name is G.G. and she's ashamed
> Because all her friends look white, brown, or gray!
> She cried because she looks this way.
> She had few friends, most ran away.
> I told her she was sunny and bright—
> A special bear with great inner light!
> Now she feels proud. All her friends know
> She's special because of her radiant glow.
> —T. R. Radd

How did the bear feel at the beginning of the poem?

How did the bear feel at the end of the poem?

Materials:

None

Explain the reasons he felt differently.

Explain a time you helped someone choose to change the way he or she felt?

Tell some ways you might help someone choose to change the way he or she feels.

www.allsucceed.com

- Other Awareness -

THE IMPACT OF AGGRESSION

Purpose: Help students learn to define and describe feelings related to personal experiences with others.

Tell the students:

> It is important that we know the way we feel about others and understand ways of explaining those feelings. This activity helps us learn ways of doing that. Please listen, follow directions, and participate.

Have a group discussion about aggressive behavior and define it to the class: "Behavior aimed at injuring some person or object, or behavior that would affect another person in a hurtful manner." The students may show their ability to understand aggressive behavior by making a collage. The entire group could be involved in this project.

Start a collage by bringing in pictures of aggressive behavior. The students have the choice of leaving their selected pictures on the collage or updating it from time to time with new pictures or drawings. When the student brings the picture, he or she may want to tell the class the following:

1. The reason that picture was chosen.

2. What he or she thinks is the possible cause for the behavior.

3. What he or she thinks he or she would have done in a similar situation. Please explain.

Ask students to discuss the way understanding aggressive behavior can help them stay safe. Ask students to give examples and discuss situations.

Notes:

Materials:
Newspaper pictures
Other source pictures
Drawing paper
Drawing supplies

© 2003
www.allsucceed.com

Notes:

- Other Awareness -

WAYS TEACHERS HELP

Purpose: Help students to learn and acknowledge the needs of others and to behave accordingly.

Tell the students:

> It is important that we are aware of the needs of others. This activity helps us learn more about their needs. Please listen, follow directions, and participate.

Ask the students to observe teachers carefully for one day. At the end of that day, ask them to share incidents that they saw or heard that showed how teachers help students.

It may be effective to clarify these observations as well as expand the activity to ask the students to illustrate the incidents they witnessed on the playground, in the cafeteria, hall, or classroom.

These illustrations can be displayed in a central location where other groups can share them.

Ask students to determine ways the teacher helped others that needed the help.

Materials:
Drawing paper
Drawing supplies

- Other Awareness -

CONCERNS SURVEY

Purpose: Help students to learn and acknowledge the needs of others and to behave accordingly.

Tell the students:

It is important that we are aware of the needs of others. This activity helps us learn more about their needs. Please listen, follow directions, and participate.

Suggest that the class devise a simple questionnaire dealing with worries or concerns. Questions could cover the following:

1. what a person is concerned about
2. how concerned he or she is
3. what he or she is no longer concerned about
4. how he or she reacts in stressful situations
5. anything else that deals with the subject and is of interest to the group

The opening question might be designed in ways that would best fit the age of the people to be questioned. The students could ask the questions of the following people:

1. students not in their class but within two years of their age
2. people older than they but under twenty-one
3. others determined by the group

The results could be arranged in a chart on the board from which the class could analyze their findings. Stress that the results of such a survey covers only a small sampling and cannot be used to make generalizations or conclusions.

Notes:

Materials:

None

Notes:

- Other Awareness -

THE IMPACT OF FEELINGS

Purpose: Help students learn to define and describe feelings related to personal experiences with others.

Tell the students:

> It is important that we know the way we feel about others and understand ways of explaining those feelings. This activity helps us learn ways of doing that. Please listen, follow directions, and participate.

Have a "feelings" board that may include the following:

- pictures representing a feeling to be identified and discussed

- the students' artistic portrayals of their feelings

- a blank area where students or leaders may make a spontaneous drawing of feelings they need to release

A board can provide the students with a constant reminder to think about what feelings may be affecting their own and other students' behaviors.

Change the pictures on the board to correlate with the feeling being discussed as the groups needs change. Ask students to discuss their observations of the changes they observe and experience.

Materials:

Drawing paper
Drawing supplies

© 2003
www.allsucceed.com

Notes:

- Other Awareness -

INCLUDING OTHERS

Purpose: Help students learn to define and describe feelings related to personal experiences with others.

Tell the students:

> It is important that we know the way we feel about others and understand ways of explaining those feelings. This activity helps us learn ways of doing that. Please listen, follow directions, and participate.

Discuss with the group the reasons students sometimes are rejected from groups. Do not talk about specific students.

Suggestions might include:

> They are slow.
> They act too smart.
> They dress differently.
> They cheat.
> They have a handicap.
> They are of a different nationality.
> They always want to be first.
> They are bossy.
> They get others into trouble.
> Other suggestions determined by the group.

Have the students identify reasons for exclusion which they believe are valid and reasons which they believe are not valid.

During the discussion of characteristics that seem to justify exclusion, explore possibilities of helping the excluded student become a more effective group member.

Materials:

None

Notes:

- Other Awareness -

NEED FOR SAFETY

Purpose: Help students learn to define and describe feelings related to personal experiences with others.

Duplicate and distribute the Need For Safety activity sheet. Introduce ways of satisfying security needs, such as:

1. knowing we can take care of our needs
2. knowing we are safe
3. knowing we are liked
4. knowing we can do things well
5. knowing we belong to a group
6. knowing we will not lose something that helps us choose to feel secure

Have the students plan to interview, first a student from the group, then an older friend or some member of the family, and ask:

1. When do you feel secure or safe?

2. When you do not feel secure about something, what do you do?

3. What were you afraid of when you were younger?

4. Which fears did you take care of as you grew older?

5. Which of these fears are still with you?

6. Do you have any new fears now that you are older?

Materials:

Activity sheet

Ask students to discuss their findings with the group. Determine ideas that may be helpful in life situations.

© 2003
www.allsucceed.com

142

- Activity sheet -

Need for Safety

Interview, first a student from your group, then an older friend or some member of the family, and ask:

1. When do you feel secure or safe?
   Student: _____
   Older person: _____

2. When you do not feel secure about something, what do you do?
   Student: _____
   Older person: _____

3. What were you afraid of when you were younger?
   Student: _____
   Older person: _____

4. Which fears did you take care of as you grew older?
   Student: _____
   Older person: _____

5. Which of these fears are still with you?
   Student: _____
   Older person: _____

6. Do you have any new fears now that you are older?
   Student: _____
   Older person: _____

Notes:

- Other Awareness -

COMMUNICATING GESTURES

Purpose: Help students learn the nonverbal communication of others.

Duplicate the Communicating Gestures activity sheet. Cut the gesture communication squares and put them in a container. You may add gestures in the blank squares or ask the students to add their own if they pull a blank square from the container. Ask for a volunteer to select and imitate the gesture.

1. clenched fist (Anger)
2. blowing a kiss (Affection)
3. clapping hands (Appreciation)
4. shaking finger (Displeasure)
5. stroking one index finger with the other (Shame)
6. patting stomach (Enjoyment)
7. holding nose (Displeasure)
8. tapping finger (Boredom)
9. fingers in ears (Displeasure)
10. arms and hands straight overhead (Success)

After each imitation, ask the following questions:

1. What feeling does this communicate to you?

2. Have you ever seen anyone use this gesture? Can you describe what was happening?

After all gestures have been considered, ask:

1. Which of these gestures communicate hurtful or helpful behaviors?

3. Please list times that we use gestures to communicate thoughts and feelings.

Materials:

Activity sheet

© 2003
www.allsucceed.com

144

- Activity sheet -

Communicating Gestures

clenched fist (anger)	blowing a kiss (affection)
clapping hands (appreciation)	shaking finger (displeasure)
stroking one index finger with the other (shame)	patting stomach (enjoyment)
holding nose (displeasure)	tapping finger (boredom)
finger in ears (displeasure)	arms and hands straight overhead (success)

Notes:

- Other Awareness -

EXPLORING GESTURES

Purpose: Help students learn the nonverbal communication of others.

Tell the students:

It is important that we know the way we feel about others and understand nonverbal ways of explaining those feelings. This activity helps us learn ways of doing that. Please listen, follow directions, and participate.

Duplicate and distribute the Communicating Gestures activity sheet on the previous page. Ask the students to recall the gestures they practiced in the Communicating Gestures activity. Use the following questions to guide further discussion:

1. Which gestures do you use most often?

2. Which gestures help you to communicate feelings without talking?

3. Which gestures do you find easier to use?

4. Which gestures do you find difficult?

5. Which gestures do you like others to use?

6. How can you know that you have communicated your feeling by gestures?

7. What are some gestures you use that probably would not be recognized by students in another school or country?

8. Can you think of some people who might communicate entirely with gestures?

9. Do you think it is important to pay attention to gestures? How important? Please explain.

Materials:
Activity sheet
Communicating Gestures

- Other Awareness -

ROLE-PLAY A HURTFUL ACTION

Purpose: Help students to learn and acknowledge the needs of others and to behave accordingly.

Tell the students:

> It is important that we are aware of the needs of others. This activity helps us learn more about their needs. Please listen, follow directions, and participate.

The effects of a behavior help us decide whether it is hurtful.

Sometimes an action may be hurtful in one situation and not in another; therefore, the students need to learn to question a behavior and its effects in order to decide how they will act.

Ask the students to role-play a hurtful action and to let the other students tell how the act was hurtful and its effects on the persons involved.

Ask students to determine ways to apply the ideas from the activity in other situations.

Notes:

Materials:
None

Notes:

- Other Awareness -

HELPFUL AND HURTFUL ACTIONS

Purpose: Help students to learn and acknowledge the needs of others and to behave accordingly.

Tell the students:

> It is important that we are aware of the needs of others. This activity helps us learn more about their needs. Please listen, follow directions, and participate.

Ask the students to draw or paint pictures showing helpful and hurtful actions and their effects. Each student can show his or her pictures to the class and tell what is happening.

The student needs to explain the reasons the action is helpful or hurtful and how the people involved might feel.

The pictures can be displayed on a board developed specifically for this purpose

Materials:

Drawing paper
Drawing supplies
Optional:
  Paint

Notes:

- Other Awareness -

FEELING SITUATIONS

Purpose: Help students learn to define and describe feelings related to personal experiences with others.

Tell the students:

It is important that we know the way we feel about others and understand ways of explaining those feelings. This activity helps us learn ways of doing that. Please listen, follow directions, and participate.

Listed below are sentences that describe a situation. Give a word that describes the feeling being expressed by the character in each situation. Remember that a situation can express more than one feeling. If students give responses that you do not understand, don't express dissatisfaction. Instead, ask them to explain the reasons they believe that the situation expresses such a feeling. Read the sentences and ask students to write their responses. Ask students to discuss their answers.

1. Rosa's dad gives her a kiss. How do you think she felt?

2. A rabbit hops with all his might to get away from a dog. If he feels the way people do, how do you think he feels?

3. James is moving far away. How does he feel?

4. Miesha has a new baby brother. How might she feel?

5. Bob is having a bad dream and wakes up crying. How might he feel?

6. Ricardo is lost in a large store. How do you think he feels?

7. Aparna has taught herself to swim. How does she feel?

Materials:

Optional:
Feeling Words Lists on pages 293-295

Notes:

- Other Awareness -

HURTFUL ACTIONS IN FAIRY TALES

Purpose: Help students learn to define and describe feelings related to personal experiences with fairy tales.

Tell the students:

> It is important that we know the way we feel about others and understand ways of explaining those feelings. This activity helps us learn ways of doing that. Please listen, follow directions, and participate.

First, define a fairy tale, then read one to the class (e.g., *Hansel and Gretel, Jack and the Beanstalk, The Three Little Pigs*, or Little *Red Riding Hood*). As you read, the individuals can raise their hands whenever they recognize a hurtful action. Stop reading and ask the following questions about that action:

1. For what reason is it harmful?

2. Whom does it hurt?

3. For what reason does this hurtful action occur?

4. What is another way the person can act without harming someone?

5. Tell the group if the story scared you. Do you like to be scared?

Materials:
Fairy tales

When you finish reading the tale, ask the group to make up a new ending that does not involve hurtful actions. The students can tell how the character's needs can be satisfied in ways that don't harm others.

- Other Awareness -

GUESS THE FEELING

Purpose: Help students learn to define and describe feelings related to personal experiences with others.

Tell the students:

> It is important that we know the way we feel about others and understand ways of explaining those feelings. This activity helps us learn ways of doing that. Please listen, follow directions, and participate.

Ask the students to play the game, "Guess the Feeling."

Duplicate and cut the Feeling Words Cards activity sheets.

Divide the students into groups.

Ask each group to act out a feeling. Other groups get three attempts to guess what the feeling is.

The groups take turns acting out the feelings.

Optional: Ask each small group to write a short story incorporating their feeling demonstrations into one story.

Notes:

Materials:

Activity sheet Feeling Words Cards on pages 296-305

Notes:

- Other Awareness -

FEELING WORD COMMUNICATION

Purpose: Help students learn to define and describe feelings related to personal experiences with others.

Duplicate and distribute the appropriate Feeling Words Lists and Feeling Words Cards activity sheets beginning on page 293.

Divide the class into two teams. Have the teams count off and flip a coin to decide which team will be first.

Have the first player choose a word from the activity sheets and whisper it to you. Make sure the student understands the meaning of the word. If necessary, ask the student to choose another word that is understood.

Then ask the student to make up a descriptive phrase or sentence which communicates that feeling word. Synonyms, gestures, and postures may be used to help to communicate the word, but the player may not say the word (e.g., "Gosh, I sure do miss everybody.").

Within 30 seconds, the player's team is to guess the feeling word; and if they do, the team gets one point.

If a player forgets and uses the actual word, he or she loses that turn.

Ask teams to alternate turns.

Optional: Ask teams to help each other solve the feeling challenge and split the points for cooperating.

Materials:

Feeling Words Lists and Cards

Notes:

- Other Awareness -

EXPANDING FEELING VOCABULARY

Purpose: Help students learn to define and describe feelings related to personal experiences with others.

Tell the students:

> It is important that we know the way we feel about others and understand ways of explaining those feelings. This activity helps us learn ways of doing that. Please listen, follow directions, and participate.

Duplicate and distribute the appropriate Feeling Words Lists activity sheets beginning on page 293. Ask each student to draw a large tic-tac-toe grid on a full sheet of paper. Ask students to choose nine words from the list and write one of the words in each square of the grid. Use the board to illustrate.

For the first round, hold up either a feeling picture for 10 seconds. With a chip or small square of construction paper, each student is to mark the feeling on his or her paper that best describes the feeling illustrated.

Continue this procedure until someone calls out "tic-tac-toe." Any combination of three words down, across or diagonally wins. Do not stress accuracy in this game.

For subsequent rounds, select other illustrations at random and reduce the time each one is shown to 5 seconds.

Materials:
Feeling pictures
Paper
Pencil
Chips or squares of paper
Activity sheet

© 2003
www.allsucceed.com

Notes:

- Other Awareness -

BEING NEW

Purpose: Help students learn to appreciate both their own feelings and the feelings of others.

Duplicate and distribute the Being New activity sheet.

This activity will help students begin to understand and appreciate both their own feelings and those of others. The exercise could provide the background understanding which the students need in order to handle school situations casually.

Have the students complete the following:

1. Have you ever been a newcomer? How did you feel?
   _____

2. Tell two ways or ideas a newcomer might use to make friends.
   _____
   _____

3. What are some ways or ideas you might use to make friends with a newcomer? _____
   _____

Ask the students to use the Creative Corner to draw or express ways or ideas they might use to make friends with a newcomer.

Materials:

Activity sheet

 © 2003
www.allsucceed.com

- Activity sheet -

Being New

Complete the following:

1. Have you ever been a newcomer? How did you feel?
   _____.

2. Tell two ways or ideas a newcomer might use to make friends.
   _____
   _____

3. What are some ways or ideas you might use to make friends with a newcomer? _____
   _____

Use the Creative Corner to draw or express ways or ideas you might use to make friends with a newcomer.

```
C r e a t i v e
o
r
n
e
r
```

Notes:

- Other Awareness -

HURTFUL BEHAVIORS

Purpose: Help students to learn and acknowledge the needs of others and to behave accordingly.

Tell the students:

> It is important that we are aware of the needs of others. This activity helps us learn more about their needs. Please listen, follow directions, and participate.

Before beginning, send home a letter which explains to parents that the class is studying hurtful behaviors shown on TV.

One evening students can watch TV and tell their parents how many times they see a "hurtful behavior." The parents can help count and sort out behaviors that might be hurting someone. Do not make this a competitive activity.

Another day, ask the students to keep a tally of the number of times they see hurtful behaviors on TV, at home, or on the playground. After completing their observations, the discussion can revolve around whether people like to watch others get hurt. Ask the following questions:

> Can you explain the reasons some people like to see others get hurt?
>
> Do most people like to watch this type of behavior? Please explain.
>
> Can you think of some reasons there might be so much hurtful behavior?

Materials:

None

© 2003
www.allsucceed.com

- Other Awareness -

GUESS THEIR ANSWERS

Notes:

Purpose: Help students learn to define and describe feelings related to personal experiences with others.

Tell the students:

> It is important that we know the way we feel about others and understand ways of explaining those feelings. This activity helps us learn ways of doing that. Please listen, follow directions, and participate.

Often people feel they know how another person feels about certain issues. This activity examines the validity of that feeling.

Instruct each student to pair with another, then write on the board some statements of opinion.

Each student is to give his or her own answers and the answers he or she believes his or her partner will give. Ask students to write these separately and then exchange papers to see how well they judged their partners' answers.

The pairs would be given time after each statement to discuss the reason they guessed correctly or incorrectly.

There are two important phases of communication going on here. One phase shows what the words of the sentence actually communicate to the person. The second phase shows what the students do that enables them to guess their partners' response.

Possible opinion statements include the following:

1. Wars are necessary.
2. Girls or women are smarter than boys or men.
3. Everyone needs a best friend.
4. Boys or men make better leaders than girls or women.
5. People cannot change their behavior.

Materials:

None

© 2003
www.allsucceed.com

Notes:

- Other Awareness -

ASSERTION AND AGGRESSION PROJECTS

Purpose: Help students learn and acknowledge the difference between assertive and aggressive behavior when they communicate with others.

Tell the students:

> It is important that we are aware of the difference between assertive and aggressive behavior and the impact those behaviors have on others. This activity helps us learn more about the impact. Please listen, follow directions, and participate.

Have a discussion about assertive and aggressive behaviors and define the differences with the students.

1. Aggressive behavior is aimed at injuring some person or object or behavior which would affect another person in a hurtful manner.
2. Assertive behavior is aimed at asking for what one wants in a timely and appropriate manner in contrast to either passive or aggressive behaviors.

The students may show their ability to understand assertive and aggressive behaviors by doing individual or group projects. Below is a list of examples:

1. Act out a form of aggression and assertion.
2. Recite poems or plays which depict aggression and assertion.
3. Bring and play music tapes or CD's which talk of aggression and assertion.
4. Write stories or poems about aggression and assertion.
5. Draw sketches or cartoons illustrating aggression and assertion.

Materials:
None

Share and discuss these examples with the group. Point out the benefits of assertive behavior. Ask students to discuss the differences and the impact of both behavior choices on the other students.

© 2003
www.allsucceed.com

- Other Awareness -

PROBLEM EXPERIENCES

Purpose: Help students to learn and acknowledge the needs of others and to behave accordingly.

Tell the students:

> It is important that we are aware of the needs of others. This activity helps us learn more about their needs. Please listen, follow directions, and participate.

Read the following paragraphs to the class. After each one, give the students time to write suggestions for helping alleviate the problem stated.

1. When Sophia was a little girl, her brother used to tell her that if she were bad, the bogeyman would get her. She slept with the light on after that. Now Sophia is 12 and still is afraid of the dark.

2. Miquel loved the water. All of his friends called him "the fish". One summer day while he was swimming in the pool, Miquel dove off the high board, even though he'd never learned how. He landed smack on his belly and got a bad stomach burn. Now he can't bring himself to dive again.

3. Deepak, at 7, saw a truck run over his dog. Since then, he has had a strong dislike for trucks and truck drivers.

Ask the group to discuss their suggested solutions to the problems.

Discuss the different feelings students may have in each situation.

Notes:

Materials:
None

© 2003
www.allsucceed.com

Notes:

- Other Awareness -

FEELING COMPARISONS GAME

Purpose: Help students learn to define and describe feelings related to personal experiences with others.

Duplicate and distribute the Feeling Comparisons Game activity sheet. Divide the students into small groups. Ask students to point to the feeling face that shows their feelings as you ask the students the following questions. Then, ask the students to check with their group members for similarities and differences in their answers. Add other examples as is appropriate for the group.

How does it feel when you:

    smile at someone?

    laugh at someone?

    make friends with someone?

    leave someone out of the game?

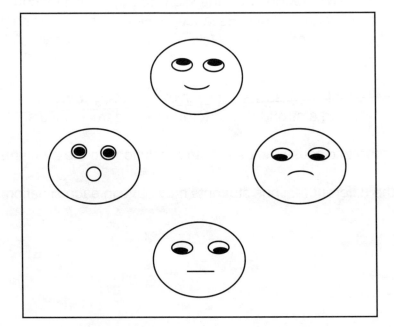

Materials:

Activity sheet

- Activity sheet -

Feeling Comparisons Game

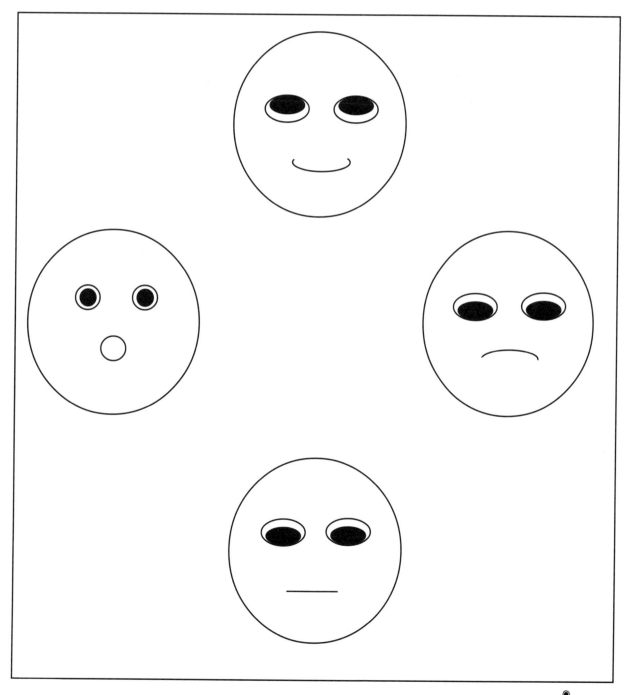

SELF-CONTROL

Self-Control:

An awareness of personal limitations and needs, and the extent to which a person can assess abilities and skills.

An awareness of one's ability to set and remain within limits or boundaries and established behavior.

An ability to display acceptable behavior.

- Self-Control -

WHAT WOULD YOU DO?

Purpose: Help students learn to control themselves in difficult situations.

Tell the students:

> Practice helps us learn ways to control ourselves. This activity gives us practice. Please listen, follow directions, and participate.

This activity may be oral or written. List the following situations on the board. The group or a student selects one situation to discuss or write about. Use the questions below the situations for the basis of the writing or discussion.

1. Your little brother scribbled on your finished homework.
2. You had to clean the basement, although the other kids went off to play.
3. You found one of the neighborhood bullies picking on your little brother.
4. Your sister got up early and wore the blouse you had planned to wear.
5. Your teacher told you to be quiet; other people were talking louder than you.
6. You discovered someone had let the air out of your bike tires.

Questions:

1. What would be your first reaction in the situation you chose?
2. How could you react with a constructive expression of anger? Nonconstructive?
3. What short-term effect might your anger have upon the person(s) in each situation listed? Long-term effect?
4. How might the way you expressed anger affect you? Now? Later?

Notes:

Materials:
None

© 2003
www.allsucceed.com

Notes:

- Self-Control -

SEEING MY FUTURE

Purpose: Help students understand the importance of self-control and life success.

Duplicate and distribute the Seeing My Future activity sheet.

Have a discussion on abilities, talents, and careers; the importance of developing these abilities and talents early in life; and how career choices affect an individual's whole life. After the discussion, have the students complete the following open-ended sentences:

Ten years from now, I will be _____.

I liked these things when I was 5 years old:
1. _____ 2. _____ 3. _____

I liked these things when I was 7 years old:
1. _____ 2. _____ 3. _____

I like these things now:
1. _____ 2. _____ 3. _____

I wanted to be these things when I was 5:
1. _____ 2. _____ 3. _____

I wanted to be these things when I was 7:
1. _____ 2. _____ 3. _____

I want to be these things now:
1. _____ 2. _____ 3. _____

When I grow up I want to be:
1. _____ 2. _____ 3. _____

Discuss these completed sentences with the class. Ask students the way self-control will determine the probability of reaching your goals.

Materials:

Activity sheet

- Activity sheet -

Seeing My Future

Ten years from now, I will be_____.

I liked these things when I was 5 years old:

1. _____
2. _____
3. _____

I liked these things when I was 7 years old:

1. _____
2. _____
3. _____

I like these things now:

1. _____
2. _____
3. _____

I wanted to be these things when I was 5:

1. _____
2. _____
3. _____

I wanted to be these things when I was 7:

1. _____
2. _____
3. _____

I want to be these things now:

1. _____
2. _____
3. _____

When I grow up I want to be:

1. _____
2. _____
3. _____

Grow with Guidance® © 2003
www.allsucceed.com

Notes:

- Self-Control -

DEVELOPING SELF-DISCIPLINE

Purpose: Help students learn appropriate behaviors needed for self-discipline.

Tell the students:

> Practice helps us learn ways to control ourselves. This activity gives us practice. Please listen, follow directions, and participate.

Discuss with the class the importance of personal dignity and establishing behaviors that can be strengthened through self-discipline. Give the class the following examples of self-discipline (or they can choose one of their own), and let them strengthen that particular self-discipline behavior:

1. making contracts with the teacher for work to be performed and submitted at a particular date

2. observing a classroom rule for a specific period of time

3. doing things because they are helpful toward self and others

Allow students to brainstorm additional ideas and examples of self-discipline. Ask students to discuss their feelings about self and others when students have self-discipline.

Ask students to brainstorm strategies for improving self-discipline and apply one strategy to a life situation. Students may draw or write a story about the strategy for improvement they select.

Materials:
Optional:
 Drawing paper
 Drawing supplies

Notes:

- Self-Control -

PERSONAL REFLECTION

Purpose: Help students learn the relationship between self-control, helpful choices, and consequences.

Tell the students:

> It helps us to learn ways our self-control impacts our choices and consequences when we think back and reflect. This activity gives us a chance to do that. Please listen, follow directions, and participate.

To get students involved in evaluating the results of their own choices, ask students to write an account of a situation in which they now feel they made a hurtful choice. Ask students to explain the reason they think it was not the best choice. Would they act differently in a future situation? Please explain.

Accounts could be shared with the group if the writers are willing or if it is an assignment in composition. The topic can be limited. For example, I would have made a different choice if I had known all possibilities; I would have made a different choice if I had thought about what would happen.

Questions:

> What were my alternatives?
>
> What were the consequences of each?
>
> What would my choice be now?
>
> What consequences signaled me to change my choice?

Ask students to apply the activity ideas to various life situations.

Materials:

None

169

Notes:

- Self-Control -

GIVING COMPLEMENTS

Purpose: Help students learn strategies for demonstrating appropriate behavior.

Tell the students:

> It is important for us to learn to demonstrate appropriate behavior that helps us. This activity gives us practice. Please listen, follow directions, and participate.

Divide your class into groups of two to four each. Ask each student to relate short biographies which note the high points of their lives. The choices are to be based on what they consider to be significant from their own points of view. The listeners are asked to give sharp attention to the speaker and not to interrupt. Make sure that each speaker gets 1 full minute. When time is called, the listeners close their eyes for a moment and think of what the speaker has said. Then each of the listeners in turn will compliment the speaker on something he or she shared.

After each compliment, the speaker will respond, "Thank you, I thought you would like to know about me," or some other reply that is not a negative, hurtful response. This allows practice for the speaker to respond to a compliment in a positive manner. This continues until all persons in each group have given their biographies.

Materials:

None

- Self-Control -

BECOMING SECURE

Purpose: Help students learn strategies to develop confidence and feelings of security.

Tell the students:

> It is important for us to identify times we feel secure and insecure and learn things we can do about it. This activity gives us practice. Please listen, follow directions, and participate.

Discuss the definitions of *secure* and *insecure* with the students. Ask students to clarify the meanings and share their ideas based on their experiences.

Either in small groups or with the class, list examples of situations in which students feel secure and insecure. Examples could include the following:

1. being first to explain an assignment

2. participating in a performance

Identify reasons for each and describe ways to change the insecure situations.

Ask the students to draw a picture or write a short story about times they were secure.

Ask students to determine ways to relate ideas to life situations.

Notes:

Materials:

Optional:
Drawing paper
Drawing supplies
Paper
Pencil

Notes:

- Self-Control -

WAYS OTHERS SEE YOU

Purpose: Help students learn the way they are perceived by others.

Duplicate and distribute the Ways Others See You activity sheet.

Descriptive Words

brave	trusting	proud
confident	uncooperative	suspicious
cheerful	unlucky	selfish
disobedient	bright	stupid
friendly	bold	unselfish
impolite	cautious	unpopular
obedient	energetic	creative
popular	honest	courteous
pouty	insecure	dishonest
sassy	lazy	helpful
strong	optimistic	pessimistic
lucky	cooperative	unkind

Ask the students to cut out each word in the activity sheet. Instruct students to put into one stack all words which they feel describe the way their mother sees them. After the words are selected, have them list the words on a piece of paper under the heading, Ways Mom Sees Me. Repeat for Ways Dad Sees Me, Ways My Best Friend Sees Me, and Ways I See Myself.

Discuss:

Who sees you most closely to the way you see yourself?

Materials:

Where do your ideas about yourself come from?

Activity sheet

www.allsucceed.com

- Activity sheet -

Ways Others See You

Descriptive Words

brave	trusting	proud
confident	uncooperative	suspicious
cheerful	unlucky	selfish
disobedient	bright	stupid
friendly	bold	unselfish
impolite	cautious	unpopular
obedient	energetic	creative
popular	honest	courteous
pouty	insecure	dishonest
sassy	lazy	helpful
strong	optimistic	pessimistic
lucky	cooperative	unkind

173

Notes:

- Self-Control -

BECOMING WHAT YOU WISH

Purpose: Help students learn strategies for demonstrating appropriate behavior.

Tell the students:

> It is important to know that we can make improvements and become the persons we want to become. This activity gives us practice. Please listen, follow directions, and participate.

Ask the students to use the words from the "Ways Others See You" activity and sort the words into two stacks. Put words that describe the way they wish they were in one stack and words that describe the way they are in another.

After they have sorted them, have them write the words from each stack on a sheet of paper under the appropriate heading, "I Am" or "I Wish I Were".

When everyone has finished, say to them, "Look at the words you have written in the I Wish I Were column. Choose two of these ways you would like to be."

Allow time for students to consider their choices, then ask them what they can do to make these wishes come true.

Lead students to consider general suggestions, such as writing down goals and spending time each day working on a goal, rather than asking them to reveal their own goal.

Tell students that you will help them work toward their goals. Ask students to make a note of the goals they would like to work on and check their progress.

Materials:

Ways Others See Me activity sheet on page 173

174

Notes:

- Self-Control -

INFLUENCE OF EXPERIENCES

Purpose: Help students learn to determine ways their memories and experiences affect self-control.

Tell the students:

> It is important to know the impact our memories and experiences have on us. Then we can use these memories and experiences to affect our self-control. This activity gives us practice. Please listen, follow directions, and participate.

Ask each student to think of one of his or her most vivid memories. Some students might want to improvise a short role-play based on a remembered experience. Was the experience pleasant or unpleasant, or was it made pleasant or unpleasant by something that happened before or after the event?

Ask the student whether they think the experience influenced them in any way, and if so, how much. Did the experience change their present attitudes or interests? This might also include the questions about the reasons they remember the experience so vividly.

Ask the students to determine ways their memories and experiences affect self-control.

Materials:

None

© 2003
www.allsucceed.com

Notes:

- Self-Control -

FEELINGS AND SELF-CONTROL

Purpose: Help students learn the impact of desirable and undesirable feelings on their behavior.

Duplicate and distribute the Feelings and Self-Control activity sheet.

Feeling Words

angry	proud	silly	tired
astonished	relaxed	surprised	bored
scared	annoyed	satisfied	tense
cheerful	ashamed	miserable	eager
disgusted	anxious	critical	happy
delighted	contented	envious	sad
discouraged	excited	depressed	guilty
embarrassed	frustrated	grumpy	gloomy
irritated	indifferent	pleased	confident
interested	satisfied	loving	jealous

Ask the students to cut out and sort the words into three stacks according to whether they feel that way often, sometimes, or never. After words are sorted, ask students to write words under the appropriate headings, <u>Often</u>, <u>Sometimes</u> or <u>Never</u>. Then tell students to go through the list of feelings they have made and place an **M** (for me) if this feeling is usually directed at themselves or an **O** (for others) if this feeling is usually directed at others. Discuss feelings marked with an **M** desirable or undesirable. Do the same for **O** feelings.

Ask students to explain the way their feelings toward self and others affects their self-control.

Materials:

Activity sheet

www.allsucceed.com

176

- Activity sheet -

Feelings and Self-Control

Feeling Words

angry	proud	silly	tired
astonished	relaxed	surprised	bored
scared	annoyed	satisfied	tense
cheerful	ashamed	miserable	eager
disgusted	anxious	critical	happy
delighted	contented	envious	sad
discouraged	excited	depressed	guilty
embarrassed	frustrated	grumpy	gloomy
irritated	indifferent	pleased	confident
interested	satisfied	loving	jealous

Notes:

- Self-Control -

CHARACTERISTICS FOR STUDENT SUCCESS

Purpose: Help students to learn characteristics of successful students and to assess their abilities and skills.

Duplicate and distribute the Characteristics for Student Success activity sheet.

Divide the class into small groups and give each group the list of characteristics below. Instruct them to first select the three most important characteristics of a successful student and rate them 1, 2, 3. Then select the three least important characteristics and rate them 13, 14, 15. Share choices and reasons.

Rank	Characteristic
____	is an effective listener
____	helps others
____	respects others
____	completes work on time
____	is friendly
____	obeys rules
____	respects teachers
____	has new ideas
____	speaks clearly
____	shares ideas
____	uses free time wisely
____	is honest
____	works independently
____	behaves well
____	follows directions

Materials:

Activity sheet

Ask students to use the Creative Corner to draw or express ways of being a successful student.

www.allsucceed.com

- Activity sheet -

Characteristics for Student Success

Select the three most important characteristics of a successful student and rate them 1, 2, 3. Then select the three least important characteristics and rate them 13, 14, 15. Share choices and reasons.

Rank	Characteristic	Rank	Characteristic
____	is an effective listener	____	helps others
____	respects others	____	completes work on time
____	is friendly	____	obeys rules
____	respects teachers	____	has new ideas
____	speaks clearly	____	shares ideas
____	uses free time wisely	____	is honest
____	works independently	____	behaves well
____	follows directions		

Use the Creative Corner to draw or express ways of being a successful student.

Creative
Corner

179

Notes:

- Self-Control -

ATTITUDE SURVEY

Purpose: Help students learn the importance and benefits of following the rules.

Duplicate and distribute the Attitude Survey activity sheet.

Students may self-administer and score a survey to determine their present attitudes about rules and authority. The following items may be used:

1. I think rules are important.
2. I think rules are fair.
3. I think it is necessary to have persons with authority to interpret and enforce rules.
4. I think the teacher (principal, parent) is fair in applying rules.
5. I think it is important to know the reason for rules.
6. I think it is fair that I help set the rules that affect me.

Score these attitudes on a four-point scale (3 = always, 2 = sometimes, 1 = hardly ever, 0 = never).

Students discuss their own opinions about rules and authority with these questions in mind:

Can you explain the reasons we have rules at school? At home? In groups? For state or country?

What different feelings do we have about them? Please explain.

Materials:

Activity sheet

- Activity sheet -

Attitude Survey

1. I think rules are important.

   3 = Always   2 = Sometimes   1 = Hardly Ever   0 = Never

2. I think rules are fair.

   3 = Always   2 = Sometimes   1 = Hardly Ever   0 = Never

3. I think it is necessary to have persons with authority to interpret and enforce rules.

   3 = Always   2 = Sometimes   1 = Hardly Ever   0 = Never

4. I think the teacher (principal, parent) is fair in applying rules.

   3 = Always   2 = Sometimes   1 = Hardly Ever   0 = Never

5. I think it is important to know the reason for rules.

   3 = Always   2 = Sometimes   1 = Hardly Ever   0 = Never

6. I think it is fair that I help set the rules that affect me.

   3 = Always   2 = Sometimes   1 = Hardly Ever   0 = Never

Notes:

- Self-Control -

WORKING AT HOME

Purpose: Help students learn strategies for demonstrating appropriate behavior.

Tell the students:

> All of us have to do some things we don't like to do. Have there been times when your parents have asked you to do some work around the house that you don't like doing? This activity gives us practice on ways to handle those situations.

Ask the students to write a story describing a job you dislike doing at home. Discuss the reason you don't like it.

> What is the reason you think you were asked to do the job?

> If you didn't do the job, who would have to do it?

Ask for volunteers to answer the questions above and discuss them with the group. Ask students to determine ways to apply ideas generated from the activity.

Materials:

None

- Self-Control -

BECOMING A LEADER

Purpose: Help students learn strategies for demonstrating appropriate behaviors to become effective leaders.

Tell the students:

> It is important for us to learn to demonstrate appropriate behaviors that help us become effective leaders. This activity gives us practice. Please listen, follow directions, and participate.

Use the following questions to guide a discussion of students' experiences as leaders:

1. When is it easy to lead other people?

2. How do you feel when you are leading other people?

3. What are some things you like to lead? What do you like about leading in that situation?

4. What do you, as the leader, hope you can take for granted about the person or persons following you?

Ask students to discuss the role self-control plays in leadership. Determine ways to apply activity ideas to various life situations.

Notes:

Materials:
None

Notes:

- Self-Control -

NEEDS AWARENESS

Purpose: Help students become aware of personal limitations and needs.

Duplicate the Needs Awareness activity sheet. Read or explain the following:

Social needs are those needs that involve a relationship with others. At school, work, or play, people find themselves in groups. Each has a reason for being with people. Social needs include the need to belong, the need to love and be loved, the need to help others and share feelings.

A person's mental needs can influence his social needs. An individual may seek certain things from a group because of the way he needs to feel about himself. If a person likes to feel proud of himself, he will probably want to be with people who respect him.

Distribute the activity sheet.

My needs	My most important needs
1. _____	1. _____
2. _____	2. _____
3. _____	3. _____
4. _____	4. _____
5. _____	5. _____
6. _____	6. _____

Discuss the activity ideas in groups or in individual student meetings. Ask students to draw or express an important need in the Creative Corner.

Materials:

Activity sheet

© 2003
www.allsucceed.com

- Activity sheet -

Needs Awareness

My needs   **My most important needs**

1. _____   1. _____
2. _____   2. _____
3. _____   3. _____
4. _____   4. _____
5. _____   5. _____
6. _____   6. _____

Draw or express an important need in the Creative Corner.

```
Creative
o
r
n
e
r
```

Notes:

- Self-Control -

MEETING YOUR NEEDS

Purpose: Help students learn the relationships between being self-satisfied, having your needs met, and self-control.

Duplicate and distribute the Meeting Your Needs activity sheet.

In the early days of the United States, people worked long hours and had little time for anything else. Gradually, the work hours shortened and the leisure time increased. One person may choose to meet only his needs; others may wish to develop creative powers, serve mankind, and make life more satisfying. On the line in front of each statement, put a "1" if the statement deals with satisfying your basic needs, and a "2" if it helps your life become more self-satisfying.

Physical Needs:
    ___ You have enough money to buy clothes.
    ___ You have enough money to buy pizza.
    ___ You live in a nice house.
    ___ You are learning to play golf.

Mental Needs:
    ___ You have time to read a new book weekly.
    ___ You have time only to read a newspaper.
    ___ You are taking piano lessons.
    ___ You like to make decisions quickly.

Social/Emotional Needs:
    ___ You see plenty of people in school and want to stay home in the evening.
    ___ You enjoy going to the movies.
    ___ You like to travel.
    ___ You enjoy going to ball games.

Ask students to discuss the relationships between being self-satisfied, having your needs met, and self-control.

Materials:

Activity sheet

- Activity sheet -

Meeting Your Needs

In the early days of the United States, people worked long hours and had little time for anything else. Gradually, the work hours shortened and the leisure time increased. One person may choose to meet only his needs; others may wish to develop creative powers, serve mankind, and make life more satisfying. On the line in front of each statement, put a **1** if the statement deals with satisfying your basic needs, and a **2** if it helps your life become more self-satisfying.

Physical Needs:
　　___ You have enough money to buy clothes.
　　___ You have enough money to buy pizza.
　　___ You live in a nice house.
　　___ You are learning to play golf.

Mental Needs:
　　___ You have time to read a new book weekly.
　　___ You have time only to read a newspaper.
　　___ You are taking piano lessons.
　　___ You like to make decisions quickly.

Social/Emotional Needs:
　　___ You see plenty of people in school and want to stay home in the evening.
　　___ You enjoy going to the movies.
　　___ You like to travel.
　　___ You enjoy going to ball games.

Notes:

- Self-Control -

MEETING BASIC NEEDS THROUGH LEISURE

Purpose: Help students learn ways that leisure activities meet basic needs.

Duplicate and distribute the Meeting Basic Needs Through Leisure activity sheet.

Work can meet some of our individual needs. People can also meet their basic needs (social, physical, mental, and emotional) in leisure activity. Ask students to code the leisure activities as they relate to their four basic needs categories: social needs, physical needs, mental needs, emotional needs.

making furniture	golfing
bowling	playing cards
flying kites	crocheting
reading	making candles
playing baseball	fishing
bicycling	snowmobiling
riding a moped	knitting
working puzzles	playing marbles
playing basketball	going to a concert
collecting stamps	jumping rope
going to a lecture	taking a music class
working with stained glass	

Ask the students to use the activity sheet and identify which leisure activities meet each of the four basic needs' categories listed. Ask students to discuss information learned about leisure activities and meeting basic needs.

Materials:

Activity sheet

© 2003
www.allsucceed.com

- Activity sheet -

Meeting Basic Needs Through Leisure

Write the code for the basic need(s) met with each leisure activity.

S = social need   P = physical need   M = mental need   E = emotional need

Leisure Activity List

____ making furniture   ____ golfing

____ bowling   ____ playing cards

____ flying kites   ____ crocheting

____ reading   ____ making candles

____ playing baseball   ____ fishing

____ bicycling   ____ snowmobiling

____ taking a trip   ____ knitting

____ working puzzles   ____ playing marbles

____ playing basketball   ____ going to a concert

____ collecting stamps   ____ jumping rope

____ going to a lecture   ____ taking a music class

Notes:

- Self-Control -

ASSESSING YOUR INTERESTS

Purpose: Help students learn strategies for assessing abilities and skills.

Duplicate and distribute the Assessing Your Interests activity sheet.

Tell the students:

> Finding areas of interest can aid self-understanding, and self-understanding can lead to beneficial career interest. This activity helps us learn more about this. Please listen, follow directions, and participate.

Ask the students to complete the activity sheet by writing or drawing their favorite sport, hobby, book, type of work, and leisure-time activity.

After the activity sheet has been completed, ask each student to give reasons for his or her choices.

Please discuss the role self-control plays in your favorite interests. In what way is self-control helpful?

Ask students to determine ways of applying activities to life situations.

Materials:

Activity sheet

© 2003
www.allsucceed.com

- Activity sheet -

Assessing Your Interests

Please write or draw your favorite:

Sport

Hobby

Book

Type of Work

Leisure-Time Activity

Notes:

- Self-Control -

HURTFUL BEHAVIORS

Purpose: Help students learn strategies for demonstrating appropriate behavior.

Tell the students:

> It is important for us to learn to demonstrate appropriate behavior that helps us. This activity gives us practice. Please listen, follow directions, and participate.

Ask the students to name some hurtful behaviors and explain the reason they are hurtful. Also, ask them to think of situations in which this action might not be hurtful and give the reasons. Below are some sample questions:

1. Is hitting a friend hurtful? Please explain.

2. How can you tell if an action is hurtful?

3. Is kicking your dog or cat hurtful? Please explain.

4. Is kicking an animal that wants to bite you hurtful? Please explain. If you did not kick him, how would you protect yourself?

5. Explain the reason an action can be hurtful in one situation and not in another?

Ask students to apply the activity ideas to other situations.

Materials:

None

© 2003
www.allsucceed.com

- Self-Control -

WHEN TO ASK FOR HELP

Purpose: Help students learn strategies for demonstrating how they can assess abilities and skills.

Tell the students:

> It is important to determine when we need help and when we can do things on our own. This activity gives us practice. Please listen, follow directions, and participate.

Discuss with the class the task of distinguishing between times they need to ask for adult help and times they could function on their own.

Examples:

1. A student comes to tell the teacher that another student has fallen on the playground and appears to be hurt.

2. A student comes to tell the teacher that another student won't let her have a turn.

3. A student wants his mother to go with him to the library to check out a book.

4. A student wants her mother to come to a play her class is giving.

Discuss with the class which students are overdependent and which students are receiving or asking for adult help because it's genuinely needed. (Some are debatable.) Expand upon the situations as interest indicates or have students suggest new situations which may be discussed.

Notes:

Materials:

None

Notes:

- Self-Control -

DREAMS OF THE FUTURE

Purpose: Help students learn strategies for reaching dreams and ambitions.

Tell the students:

> It is important for us to learn to demonstrate appropriate behavior that helps us accomplish things we want to do. This activity gives us practice. Please listen, follow directions, and participate.

Tell the class that most people have some ambitions or dreams about the future, even though they may not have told anyone about them. Encourage students to think about their dreams or ambitions and to write a few sentences beginning with, "Someday I would like . . ."

When everyone has finished, ask if anyone would like to share his or her ambition or dream with the rest of the class. Discuss the dreams and ambitions when appropriate.

Then ask the following:

1. Have you had these dreams or ambitions for a long time?

2. Do your dreams or ambitions ever change? In what ways?

3. Do you prefer to share your dreams or to keep them private?

4. How might you make dreams about the future come true?

Please ask the students to determine three ways self-control is important to reach your dreams.

Materials:
None

- Self-Control -

COMMUNICATING PROGRESS

Purpose: Help students learn ways to communicate strengths, needs, abilities, and skills.

Tell the students:

> It is important for us to learn to communicate our progress in a way that helps us. This activity gives us practice. Please listen, follow directions, and participate.

School grades are very complex symbols. They mean one thing to teachers, another to parents, and something else still to the students.

Without having the class analyze all the meanings of their grading system, it might be interesting to have them create a set of evaluation symbols they would like to use in their class.

To put students as ease, set up a fantasy situation where everyone suddenly forgot what report cards look like and how they are used to tell parents about students' work.

It could be the job of the class, as individuals or in small groups, to create a new report card that includes a clear and useful code for telling parents the important aspects of their children's progress in school. In this way, the students would have to think about what information they feel is important enough to be evaluated and in what ways the information could be communicated.

Ideally, the class could work out a master report card form that could be used and that parents could react to.

Notes:

Materials:
None

Notes:

- Self-Control -

DESCRIBE YOURSELF

Purpose: Help students learn the importance of knowing their abilities, interests, attitudes, and character qualities.

Tell the students:

> It is important for us to discover our abilities, interest, attitudes, and character qualities. This activity gives us practice. Please listen, follow directions, and participate.

Discuss with the class group (or individually) the importance of knowing our own abilities, interests, attitudes, and character qualities.

Direct the class to make a list of traits that "you think best describe you".

Then do the following:

1. List those things that can be changed.

2. List those things that cannot be changed.

3. Using the list of things that can be changed, list strong qualities and those that need strengthening separately.

4. Draw a plan of action that will help you become what you desire to be.

Materials:

None

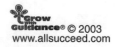

196

Notes:

- Self-Control -

SPECIAL JOB ROLE-PLAY

Purpose: Help students learn strategies for demonstrating appropriate work behavior.

Tell the students:

> It is important for us to learn to demonstrate appropriate work behavior that helps us. This activity gives us practice. Please listen, follow directions, and participate.

Have a class discussion on the importance and dignity of work. Let each student role-play something he or she does at home to help. Ask students to explain the reason doing it is important to him or her and to the family.

Begin by saying:

> Each of us has a responsibility or a special job, either at home or at school. Our jobs need to help us feel useful. Think of a special job you have. Act it out and we'll see if we can guess what it is.

Ask students or student groups to respond to the different role plays. Determine the impact self-control plays in each situation.

Optional: You may let each student role-play something he or she does at school and at other settings to help.

Materials:

None

Notes:

- Self-Control -

HANDLING RESTLESSNESS

Purpose: Help students learn strategies to control themselves in difficult situations.

Tell the students:

> Practice helps us learn ways to control ourselves. This activity gives us practice. Please listen, follow directions, and participate.

Discuss with the class how people feel when they have been sitting for a long time.

Play the song-game, *Did you Ever See a Lassie?* Have the students demonstrate restlessness in answer to the question posed in the song. Then ask them to demonstrate helpful ways to deal with the need for activity.

Some helpful and hurtful ways may be brought out in dealing with their restlessness. Through discussion, the group may decide which activities best fit into the physical classroom and the classroom atmosphere. Then ask the students which activities best fit into the out-of-doors.

The students may offer personal examples of times they've been restless and suggest what they could do in these situations. It may be helpful to add to the list and post illustrative pictures from magazine or student drawings to refer to during the year.

Materials:
Drawing paper
Drawing supplies
 or magazine
 pictures
Song: *Did You Ever See a Lassie?*

© 2003
www.allsucceed.com

198

- Self-Control -

MIRROR PERSON

Purpose: Help students learn awareness of personal limitations and needs.

Tell the students:

> It is important for us to know more information about ourselves and ways our behavior helps us. This activity gives us practice. Please listen, follow directions, and participate.

Read to the class the following poem which is designed to get students to begin to look at their own self-characteristics and self-control.

> Who's that mirror person in front of me?
> I don't understand all that I see.
> Am I quiet or yak-yak-yak?
> Am I thin or am I fat?
> Can I sit still or always move?
> Am I dull or in the groove?
> Can I ask for what I need,
> Or is that something I can't see?
> —T. R. Radd

Ask the students to listen as you read the poem. Ask students to answer each poem question in sequence as your reread it. You may wish to discuss the purposes of a mirror before you ask for answers to the questions.

Related activities:

1. Make use of concave or convex mirrors and ask the following questions. Are you really different because you now look different?

2. Look at yourself in the mirror. Draw yourself.

3. Discuss the way our self-characteristics can sometimes affect self-control.

Notes:

Materials:

Mirror
Optional:
  Concave or
  convex mirror

199

Notes:

- Self-Control -

ASSESSING CHANGE

Purpose: Help students learn ways they have changed over time.

Duplicate and distribute the Assessing Change activity sheet. Have a group discussion about how sometimes people change without knowing it.

	First Grade	Now	
		Same	Dif
Game you played			
Toy you played with			
TV show you watched			
Book you read			
Friend you had			
Where you lived			

Next to each item, write a word that tells what you did in first grade. Under the "Now" column, mark an X below "Same" if you still do this or "Dif" if you do something different or if the situation is different for you now.

Ask students to use the Creative Corner to draw or express changes and the role self-control plays.

Materials:

Activity sheet

© 2003
www.allsucceed.com

- Activity sheet -

Assessing Change

Next to each item, write a word that tells what you did in First Grade. Under the "Now" column, mark an X below "Same" if you still do this or "Dif" if you do something different or if the situation is different for you now.

	First Grade	Now	
		Same	Dif
Game you played			
Toy you played with			
TV show you watched			
Book you read			
Friend you had			
Where you lived			

C r e a t i v e
o
r
n
e
r

Notes:

- Self-Control -

EVALUATING YOUR WORK

Purpose: Help students learn strategies for evaluating and improving their work.

Tell the students:

> It is important for us to learn ways to evaluate and improve our own work. This activity gives us practice. Please listen, follow directions, and participate

This activity encourages students to evaluate and improve their own work. Show the group a few of the seals of approval found in magazine ads and on manufactured products such as the Good Housekeeping and the UL seal.

Discuss with students the meaning of such seals. Have each student design his or her own seal of approval (see illustration). Help each student design a chart outlining appropriate standards for him or herself. The standards need to be realistic (e.g., neatness, completeness, thoroughness, promptness). When the student hands in work that meets the standards, he or she can place the seal of approval on the work. Discuss the reason a seal cannot be used indiscriminately (it will lose its meaning and the student will lose the privilege of using it). Have the group keep track of how many times each week they hand in assignments bearing their seal.

Materials:

None

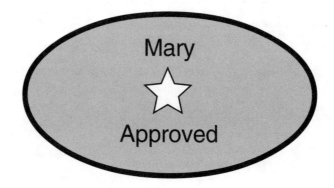

- Self-Control -

HOME RESPONSIBILITIES

Purpose: Help students learn strategies for demonstrating appropriate behavior.

Tell the students:

> It is important for us to learn to demonstrate appropriate behavior that helps us. This activity gives us practice. Please listen, follow directions, and participate

Discuss with the class how to cooperate at tasks, thus avoiding quarreling over certain situations because of a lack of cooperation.

Have students develop a personal "My Jobs" chart listing home responsibilities, such as:

> I straightened my room before bedtime.

> I picked up my clothes without being told.

> I fed the fish without being reminded.

Students may add to their charts as other jobs are accomplished.

Discuss the relationships between completing jobs, responsibility, and self-control.

Notes:

Materials:

Paper
Pencil

Notes:

- Self-Control -

WHAT'S YOUR GUESS?

Purpose: Help students learn strategies to control themselves in difficult situations.

Tell the students:

Practice helps us learn ways to control ourselves. This activity gives us practice. Please listen, follow directions, and participate.

Discuss with the class what would happen in the following situations if:

There was no school patrol to tell them when to cross the street.

There was no referee at a basketball game or umpire at a baseball game.

There were no rules for playing games.

There was no conductor to lead an orchestra.

1. Have several students role-play the different situations mentioned above and discuss the importance of behaving in a controlled manner in these situations.

2. Have students think of other situations of this kind and describe the results.

Relate the activity ideas to other life situations.

Materials:

None

- Self-Control -

CONTROL YOUR EMOTIONS

Purpose: Help students learn strategies to control themselves in difficult situations.

Tell the students:

> Practice helps us learn ways to control ourselves. This activity gives us practice. Please listen, follow directions, and participate.

Discuss with the class group how all persons have feelings and emotions. (Show pictures of students expressing different kinds of emotions.) Use selected feeling words from the Feeling Words Cards found beginning on page 296.

Discuss the importance of learning how to control and express feelings and emotions in a manner that will benefit both themselves and others. Direct students to complete the open-ended sentence:

> The feeling that is hardest for me to control is _____.

Allow other students to suggest how that emotion can be controlled.

Notes:

Materials:
Activity sheet:
  Feeling Words Cards
Optional:
  Feeling pictures

Notes:

- Self-Control -

WAYS OTHERS INFLUENCE BEHAVIOR

Purpose: Help students learn strategies to control themselves in different situations.

Tell the students:

> Practice helps us learn ways to control ourselves in different situations. This activity gives us practice. Please listen, follow directions, and participate.

To show how one behaves differently because of the presence of different people, a student might perform a simple activity like telling a joke or suggesting one that he or she would like to act out.

The student might perform for the rest of the group several times, with the group pretending to be something different each time (e.g., friends, a group of teachers and the principal, the police, parents, grandparents, or the school custodian).

Ask the students to use their imagination so that the exercise becomes as real as possible.

Find out the reasons the student acted differently each time.

> Did he or she feel stifled, uninhibited or something else?

> Explore ways students feel when behaving differently with different people.

> Explain the way that the different experiences affect self-control.

Materials:
None

- Self-Control -

THE IMPACT OF RULES

Purpose: Help students learn strategies to control themselves in difficult situations.

Tell the students:

> Practice helps us learn ways to control ourselves. This activity gives us practice. Please listen, follow directions, and participate.

Role-play or discuss the following situations:

1. Some students were playing with Legos at free time. They did not put them all away. Later, when the students were skipping, they did not see a wheel on the floor. What might have happened?

2. The class is waiting for story time and some students are playing instead of putting away their paints. What happens then?

3. A student is running down the hall from the library when a teacher from another class comes out and stops him. What will probably happen next?

Ask students to determine what needs to be done to demonstrate self-control.

Notes:

Materials:
None

Notes:

- Self-Control -

HANDLING ANXIETIES

Purpose: Help students learn strategies to control themselves in anxious situations.

Tell the students:

> Practice helps us learn ways to control ourselves when we are anxious. This activity gives us practice. Please listen, follow directions, and participate.

Discuss with the class what they would do in the following anxiety-producing situations:

1. You just finished putting together a model car. A younger child comes to your house and breaks it.

2. Your mother has asked you to go to the store for groceries. On the way to the store, you lose the money.

3. Your pet cat has eaten the parakeet your friend left with you during vacation.

Students may add other situations that were anxious for them and discuss the situation with the group.

Ask students to determine appropriate self-control strategies for the situations. Discuss ways of applying activity ideas to various life situations.

Materials:

None

© 2003
www.allsucceed.com

Notes:

- Self-Control -

WAYS TO VERBALIZE ANGER

Purpose: Help students learn strategies for demonstrating appropriate behavior.

Tell the students:

It is important for us to learn to demonstrate appropriate behavior that helps us. This activity gives us practice. Please listen, follow directions, and participate.

There are various ways to express anger. The most frequent expression of anger is through verbalization. You can write the following statements on the board, encouraging discussion as to which way you would rather have someone express anger and the reason.

1. Swearing, cursing, name calling versus "I feel angry when you (walk away) because I (want you to help me)."

2. "You thief! I'm going to tell!" versus "I don't like it when you take my things without asking."

3. "Liar." versus "You didn't tell me the truth."

4. "You're a lousy hitter. Get off the team." versus "I wish you would practice hitting."

You could assign one statement to each of two students to verbalize as if they were really talking to each other. The students may have other statements to suggest.

Ask students to determine times they can use the ideas in various life situations.

Materials:

None

Notes:

- Self-Control -

CONTROLLING YOUR ACTIVITY

Purpose: Help students learn strategies for demonstrating appropriate behavior.

Tell the students:

It is important for us to learn to demonstrate appropriate behavior that helps us. This activity gives us practice. Please listen, follow directions, and participate.

Ask the students to decide which ways of dealing with the need for activity are most helpful in your particular school situations. Encourage students to work together on posters to display as reminders of helpful methods.

It is important to help the students realize that some activities that may otherwise be helpful may not conform to your school policy or physical setting. Be sure that the activities decided upon meet the needs of both you and the student. Some helpful (but not bothersome) activities that have proven effective in certain classrooms are:

1. changing positions

2. changing locations

3. getting a drink

4. chewing gum or hard candy (quietly), if appropriate

5. doodling

6. changing activities

7. taking a walk

Also, you may suggest using some of these methods outside of school to test their effectiveness. Ask students to report the results of their tests.

Materials:

Poster paper
Art supplies

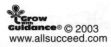
© 2003
www.allsucceed.com

- Self-Control -

THINKING CHAIR

Purpose: Help students learn strategies to control themselves in difficult situations.

Tell the students:

> Practice helps us learn ways to control ourselves. This activity gives us practice. Please listen, follow directions, and participate.

Have a "thinking chair" placed in a quiet part of the room.

If students feel that they have problems that they would like to be alone to think or talk about, they may go to the thinking chair.

Hopefully, this would provide security for students and also remove them from the group, which may be the cause of the problem or may become the brunt of the frustration. When you are free, you may ask the students if you can be of help.

Students may draw or express the solutions they think of during this thinking chair break.

Notes:

Materials:
Optional:
  Drawing paper
  Drawing supplies

Notes:

- Self-Control -

HANDLING PEER PRESSURE

Purpose: Help students learn strategies to control themselves in difficult situations.

Tell the students:

> Practice helps us learn ways to control ourselves. This activity gives us practice. Please listen, follow directions, and participate.

Discuss with the students how a group might want to pressure them into doing something they know would not be helpful in the following situations. Include in the discussions such things as the student's feelings when he is being pressured and the feelings he has if he gives into group pressure and violates his own self-control boundaries. Clarify with the students that ultimately they choose what they will do.

1. Your mom has left you at home for a little while with the instructions that no one is to come in the house while she's gone. Several friends come over and want to play with you.

2. Your brother has a new baseball and has asked you not to play with it. Some friends come over and want to play with it.

3. Your mom brought you a present from a trip. You took it to school and one of your friends coaxed and begged for you to give it to him.

Materials:
None

Students may generate other situations for the group to discuss. Ask students to determine ways that their choices demonstrate self-control and are helpful to self and others.

© 2003
www.allsucceed.com

212

- Self-Control -

HANDLING PEER PRESSURE ROLE-PLAY

Purpose: Help students learn strategies to control themselves in difficult situations.

Tell the students:

>Practice helps us learn ways to control ourselves. This activity gives us practice. Please listen, follow directions, and participate.

Ask the students to role-play or act out some of the Handling Peer Pressure situations with puppets to show how people can persuade someone to do something that is hurtful. Show both sides of the situation. In follow-up discussions, ask the students to determine who was responsible for the person's actions in each situation.

1. Your mother has left you at home for a little while with the instructions that no one is to come in the house while she's gone. Several friends come over and want to play with you.

2. Your brother has a new baseball and has asked you not to play with it. Some friends come over and want to play with it.

3. Your mother brought you a present from a trip. You took it to school and one of your friends coaxed and begged for you to give it to him.

Students may use additional situations for their role-play or puppet plays.

Optional: Students may want to make their own puppets from bags or other materials.

Notes:

Materials:

Puppets

Notes:

- Self-Control -

BEHAVIOR PROBLEMS AND SOLUTIONS

Purpose: Help students learn strategies to control themselves in difficult situations.

Tell the students:

> Practice helps us learn ways to control ourselves. This activity gives us practice. Please listen, follow directions, and participate.

Ask the students to consider possible causes for certain problem behavior and encourage them to identify more helpful reactions to each problem.

Make two sets of 3 x 5 cards.

Each card in the first set describes the kinds of behavior typical of students in that grade level (e.g., talks all the time, pushes people around, complains of illness, shows off, acts shy, acts afraid, etc.).

Each card in the second set names a possible cause for behavior (e.g., not sure of his or her ideas, would like to be stronger, doesn't think much of self, feels unliked, etc.).

Pass out cards that describe a kind of behavior to some of the students.

Place the cards that name causes for behavior on a board ledge or board.

Have each student read the behavior card he or she holds and ask another student to select a "cause card" that could help explain the behavior.

Discuss each behavior selected. Help the group identify more helpful reactions and self-control for each behavior.

Optional: Ask students to write the behavior cards in certain age levels as appropriate. Add additional cards as needed.

Materials:

3 x 5 file cards

Notes:

- Self-Control -

CHOICES AND CONSEQUENCES

Purpose: Help students learn to formulate a theory about choices and consequences and then apply it to situations.

Tell the students:

It helps us to learn ways our feelings and self-control affect our choices and consequences. This activity gives us a chance to learn and practice. Please listen, follow directions, and participate.

Ask the students to discuss the following:

Explain the meaning of choices and consequences.
(Choice: A course of action that is helpful or hurtful.)
(Consequences: Things that happen as a result of one's choices.)
Who is in charge of your choices?
Explain who determines your consequences.
Explain the way helpful choices affect your consequences.
Explain the way hurtful choices affect your consequences.

After the students have considered these questions, ask them to consider the following situations in light of their discussion. What part do feelings play in choices and consequences and in justice?

1. A student who is doing poorly in school
2. A child who never cleans his room
3. A student who is boisterous and disruptive
4. A baby who keeps crying
5. A student who is quiet and does not participate
6. A bad habit that one wants to break
7. A student who is cheating on a test
8. A person who steals something from a store

Discuss the role that self-control plays in choices and consequences.

Materials:

None

Notes:

- Self-Control -

CREATE A STORY

Purpose: Help students learn strategies for demonstrating helpful behavior.

Tell the students:

> It is important for us to learn to demonstrate behavior that helps us. This activity gives us practice. Please listen, follow directions, and participate.

Ask the students to make up a story entitled "Helpful Harry at School." Begin the story with the statement, "Once upon a time there was a boy in school whose name was Helpful Harry. These are some of the things he did."

Ask the students to contribute their ideas to complete the story. Ask them to include examples of self-control in the story they create.

Materials:
None

 © 2003
www.allsucceed.com

Notes:

- Self-Control -

NO CONFLICT ALLOWED

Purpose: Help students learn strategies to control themselves in difficult situations.

Tell the students:

> Practice helps us learn ways to control ourselves. This activity gives us practice. Please listen, follow directions, and participate.

To encourage students to broaden their view of conflict to include its creative as well as its destructive elements, ask small groups of students to think about, and then role-play, one of the following situations:

1. What would happen if no one in your family were allowed to disagree with any other family member's ideas? Show some typical family situations.

2. Show some scenes from a presidential election campaign during which all candidates agreed on all issues.

3. Supply books with fairy tales. Suppose a law were passed to prevent everyone under 5 years old from experiencing any conflict. How would you rewrite favorite stories, fairy tales, or TV shows to make them safe for preschool-aged children to hear?

4. Show us what a sport would be like if all conflict disappeared from it. What rules would be different? What would the referee do? How would the players feel? How would the fans act?

Discuss the ways that conflict can be helpful when people maintain self-control and respect for others.

Materials:

Fairy tale books

Notes:

- Self-Control -

WHAT WOULD HAPPEN?

Purpose: Help students learn strategies for demonstrating appropriate behavior.

Tell the students:

> It is important for us to learn to demonstrate appropriate behavior that helps us. This activity gives us practice. Please listen, follow directions, and participate.

Divide the class into groups and ask each group to draw a picture to show a consequence of behavior in one of the following situations:

1. A little girl left her tricycle in the street when she finished playing.

2. A boy with a new bike was showing off by riding "no hands".

3. A girl had a pet turtle that she neglected to feed for several days.

4. A boy talked back to his mother when she told him it was time to go to bed.

5. A student pushed another student out of his seat on the bus.

Discuss the role of self-control in each of these situations.

Materials:

Drawing paper
Drawing supplies

Notes:

- Self-Control -

FEELINGS IN NEW SITUATIONS

Purpose: Help students learn strategies for demonstrating appropriate behavior.

Tell the students:

> It is important for us to learn to demonstrate appropriate behavior that helps us. This activity gives us practice. Please listen, follow directions, and participate.

Have a group discussion about the different feelings we choose when confronted with new or different situations.

Ask the students to illustrate a situation and write 10 feeling words about the situation. The appropriate Feeling Words Lists and Feeling Words Cards activity sheets found beginning on page 293 may be helpful to assist students with feeling word choices.

Materials:

Drawing paper
Drawing supplies
Optional: Feeling Words activity sheets

© 2003
www.allsucceed.com

Notes:

- Self-Control -

IF THAT DOESN'T WORK . . .

Purpose: Help students learn strategies to control themselves in difficult situations.

Tell the students:

> Practice helps us learn ways to control ourselves. This activity gives us practice. Please listen, follow directions, and participate.

Civil disturbances sometimes occur when oppressed people feel that their needs have not been met and that all their alternative courses of action have been exhausted. Challenge the students to test their own frustration levels and their abilities to offer new nonviolent alternatives for unsolved problems. The class can divide into teams, and the teams might compete to plan a list of possible solutions for given problems.

These lists might be step-by-step procedures (e.g., First we would do this, and if that doesn't work . . .). The given problems might include

1. eliminating gangs from the area,

2. preventing a store from selling unfit products,

3. stopping a factory from polluting, or

4. eliminating safety hazards from school.

As appropriate, students might be encouraged to investigate the various available legal channels, nonviolent protests acts, and so on, in preparing their lists.

Materials:

Paper
Pencil

Ask students to determine possible ways to include service learning projects as a result of their investigations.

220

- Self-Control -

OWNING YOUR BEHAVIOR

Purpose: Help students learn strategies for demonstrating appropriate behavior.

Tell the students:

> It is important for us to learn to demonstrate appropriate behavior that helps us. This activity gives us practice. Please listen, follow directions, and participate.

Ask the students to tell about a time when someone "made them" get into trouble. Help students see that we always have a choice; that what we do is our own decision.

Ask students to determine the way their behavior choices and level of self-control affects what happens to them.

Students may role-play situations they have experienced.

Notes:

Materials:

None

© 2003
www.allsucceed.com

Notes:

- Self-Control -

TELLING OR TATTLING?

Purpose: Help students learn strategies for demonstrating appropriate behavior.

Tell the students:

> It is important for us to learn to demonstrate appropriate behavior that helps us. This activity gives us practice. Please listen, follow directions, and participate.

Write "telling" and "tattling" on the board. In a discussion, bring out that reporting that helps someone is <u>telling</u>, whereas reporting that does not help and may even hurt someone is <u>tattling</u>. After establishing this distinction, you could ask:

1. Have you ever heard anyone say, "I'm going to tell"? Have you ever said it? When? Has anyone ever said this to you? When? Explain your feelings.

2. Have you ever heard anyone called a tattletale? Have you ever called anyone a tattletale? Explain your feelings.

3. Explain the reason a person might tell on others. (You can list the reasons on the board.)

4. Is telling always tattling? Give examples. You might also make a situation in which the class has to decide whether the informer is telling or tattling. For example, if someone told an adult that Joe was making snowballs and throwing them at smaller students, would the informant be telling or tattling?

Have the class think of other examples.

Materials:

None

- Self-Control -

APPROPRIATE BEHAVIOR

Notes:

Purpose: Help students learn strategies for demonstrating appropriate behavior.

Tell the students:

> It is important for us to learn to demonstrate appropriate behavior that helps us. This activity gives us practice. Please listen, follow directions, and participate.

Organize a short trip to an expensive restaurant, yet one where the class could order ice cream, a soft drink, or something relatively inexpensive.

Note: Prearrange this trip with the restaurant management and invite adults to accompany the group. If a field trip is not feasible, the restaurant situation might be simulated in the room.

Before students have the trip experience, discuss ways that appropriate behavior differs from place to place and is strictly observed.

After students return, ask students the differences they observed between student behavior in the classroom or the home, on the trip, and when they returned to the classroom. One may act different in his own home than in another home. For example, state the reasons someone might be willing to help with the dishes at a friend's house but have to be coaxed to do them at home.

Materials:

None

Notes:

- Self-Control -

TALK IT OVER

Purpose: Help students learn strategies to develop confidence and feelings of security.

Tell the students:

> It is important for us to identify times we feel secure and insecure and learn things we can do about it. This activity gives us practice. Please listen, follow directions, and participate.

Discuss with the students or student the effects that the emotions of fear, anger, and worry have on feelings of security and on the appetite and digestion.

Explain that talking over a problem or fear with parents, a counselor, or a teacher can prevent upset stomachs or a feeling of insecurity. This procedure often brings peace of mind and a feeling of relaxation.

Ask students to test this idea and report the results to the group

Materials:

None

© 2003
www.allsucceed.com

- Self-Control -

CHALLENGE BANK

Purpose: Help students learn strategies to control themselves in difficult situations.

Tell the students:

> It helps us learn ways to control ourselves when we practice. This activity gives us practice. Please listen, follow directions, and participate.

Develop a "Bank" of challenging situations that can be picked out, role-played, and discussed. Puppets can be an effective medium of expression for this or any role-playing activity. Students may feel more secure in assuming a role if they can use a puppet to portray the character.

Give students the chance to relate personal experiences about times when they felt anger.

Discuss with the students some other reasons people may become angry. Ask them to offer instances that revealed their anger.

Have the students think of different ways people act when they become angry.

Students may also volunteer to demonstrate these ways.

Notes:

Materials:

Optional:
Puppets

Notes:

- Self-Control -

GROUP PATTERN EXPERIENCE

Purpose: Help students learn the effect other peoples' behavior has on their behavior and self-control.

Tell the students:

> It is important for us to learn ways we are leaders or followers influenced by the behavior of others. This activity gives us practice.

To show how strongly group patterns might influence individual behavior, use this kind of experiment.

Early in the day, six or seven students might be asked secretly to act as confederates.

At a fixed signal, students would be expected to interrupt their work for a moment and perform, one after the other, similar actions uncommon to classroom routines.

For example, during study period in which absolute silence is expected, hand a marker to the first confederate. He would then print his name forward and backward on the board and hand the marker to the second confederate. The second would then do the same with her own name and hand the marker to the third confederate and so on. Eventually, the last confederate can hand the marker to the next student and, if the pattern has been clearly established, the rest of the class will probably continue to take turns printing their names forward and backward on the board.

This behavior is more successful if acted out by seats and rows rather than randomly.

Discuss the reason students will become followers. Explore the relationship between following and self-control.

Materials:

None

© 2003
www.allsucceed.com

- Self-Control -

HANDLE YOUR ANGER

Purpose: Help students learn strategies to control themselves in difficult situations.

Tell the students:

> Practice helps us learn ways to control ourselves. This activity gives us practice. Please listen, follow directions, and participate.

Discuss with the students how frustration is caused and how it sometimes leads to anger.

Display to the class pictures expressing anger, or ask students to demonstrate what anger might look like, sound like, and feel like.

Talk about situations where angry feelings occur and ways of controlling angry feelings caused by frustration.

Role-play the control of angry feelings when someone takes something that is yours. Tell what thoughts help to handle the angry feelings and discuss them with the class group.

Continue with other situations suggested by the students. Ask students to determine thoughts that help them maintain self-control.

Notes:

Materials:

Pictures of anger
  or
Drawing paper
Drawing supplies

Notes:

- Self-Control -

ANGER DISCUSSIONS

Purpose: Help students learn to use discussion as one way to control anger.

Duplicate and distribute the Anger Discussions activity sheet.

Discuss with the class the importance of talking about angry feelings with someone, instead of suppressing them, and learning to deal with them in a constructive way. Include in the discussion the importance of their daily decisions—what to do, what to read, what programs to watch, and so on.

Then have each student complete the following sentence:

    When I was angry, it helped me to talk with _____

    _____ because _____

    _____.

Ask for volunteers to discuss their completed sentences with the class.

The Creative Corner is provided for drawing and expressing other thoughts and feelings of these situations.

Materials:

Activity sheet

- Activity sheet -

Anger Discussions

Complete the following sentence:

When I was angry, it helped me to talk with _____
_____ because _____
_____
_____.

Draw or express other thoughts and feelings of these situations.

```
C r e a t i v e
o
r
n
e
r
```

Notes:

- Self-Control -

SENTENCE COMPLETION

Purpose: Help students learn strategies for demonstrating appropriate behavior.

Duplicate and distribute the Sentence Completion activity sheet.

The following open-ended sentences might be used for group discussion, for individual conferences or as topics for drawing or for writing paragraphs or short stories.

1. Behavior is _____.

2. The way I feel about the reason I do things is _____
   _____.

3. The way I feel when I learn the reason other people do things is _____.

4. One problem with finding the real cause for behavior is _____.

5. Some ways to find out what causes things are _____.

6. I don't understand the reason people _____
   _____.

Materials:

Activity sheet

7. Sometimes I don't understand the reason _____
   _____.

Ask students to apply the information learned to other life situations.

- Activity sheet -

Sentence Completion

1. Behavior is _____.

2. The way I feel about the reason I do things is _____
   _____.

3. The way I feel when I learn the reason other people do things is _____
   _____.

4. One problem with finding the real cause for behavior is
   _____.

5. Some ways to find out what causes things are _____
   _____.

6. I don't understand the reason people _____
   _____.

7. Sometimes I don't understand the reason I _____
   _____
   _____.

Notes:

- Self-Control -

TELEVISE SOLUTIONS

Purpose: Help students learn strategies to control themselves in difficult situations.

Tell the students:

> Practice helps us learn ways to control ourselves. This activity gives us practice. Please listen, follow directions, and participate.

Ask the students to prepare a television program by using pictures to show details that might cause fear when visiting a doctor's office, dentist's office, or when transferring to a new school.

Role-play a solution to overcome a specific fear and present the solution on the class television show. Discuss ways fear effects self-control.

Materials:
Drawing paper
Art supplies

- Self-Control -

THE IMPACT OF NEEDS ON ACTIONS

Purpose: Help students learn strategies for demonstrating appropriate behavior.

Tell the students:

It is important for us to learn to demonstrate appropriate behavior that helps us. This activity gives us practice. Please listen, follow directions, and participate.

This activity may help the students understand that unfulfilled needs can affect peoples' choices to use hurtful actions.

Make two sets of flashcards, each set on a different color of paper. On each card of one set, list a need (e.g., love, food, rest, friends, being a somebody, security, warmth, clothes).

On each card of the other set, list a hurtful action (e.g., hitting, pushing, kicking, breaking, tattling). Give a need card and a hurtful action card to each student or to a small group of students.

Ask each student to draw one picture to illustrate the hurtful action card.

When the pictures are completed, each student can tell or write a descriptive story about how the drawn need card can affect a person's choice to use a hurtful action. The students may find that a need can affect the different actions and that an action can be affected by different needs.

Optional: Ask students to write the behavior cards in certain age levels as appropriate. Add additional cards as needed.

Notes:

Materials:

Colored paper
Flash cards with needs and actions
Drawing supplies

© 2003
www.allsucceed.com

Notes:

- Self-Control -

CREATE LEARNING STORIES

Purpose: Help students learn strategies for demonstrating appropriate behavior.

Tell the students:

It is important for us to learn to demonstrate appropriate behavior that helps us. This activity gives us practice. Please listen, follow directions, and participate.

Ask the students to make up short stories to fit the following sentences:

Once upon a time there was a student who went to school. She did not listen when the teacher told about _____, so that is the reason she cannot _____.

Ask students to discuss the effect of self-control on learning. Ask them to give examples of times their self-control was helpful to their learning.

Materials:

None

- Self-Control -

ASSERTIVE BEHAVIOR

Purpose: Help students learn the impact of assertive behavior on their feelings and attitudes toward self and others.

Tell the students:

> It is important for us to learn to demonstrate appropriate behavior that helps us. This activity gives us practice in using helpful, assertive behavior. Please listen, follow directions, and participate.

Discuss the following definition of assertive behavior with the students:

> Behavior aimed at asking for what one wants in a timely and appropriate manner, in contrast to either passive or aggressive behaviors.

It is important for students to understand about assertive actions, because they can really have a positive effect on self-control. Ask students to show their ability to understand assertive behavior by making folders, individually or in a group, that would contain clippings from newspapers or magazines, or short descriptions from episodes on TV or in the movies that they think show assertive behavior.

Proceed by:
1. Distributing the materials and supplies and ask students to begin finding examples of assertive behavior.
2. Determine if the activity is to be done individually or in a group.
3. Ask students to begin searching for examples of assertive behavior and bring those examples to school by a certain date.
4. Ask students to determine their feelings and attitudes toward self and their self-control when they experience assertive behavior *or* when they are assertive.

Ask the group or individual to share and discuss their folder of assertive behavior examples with the class. Ask the class to determine what was learned from their experience.

Notes:

Materials:
Construction
 paper
Newspapers
Magazines
Art supplies
Scissors

© 2003
www.allsucceed.com

Notes:

- Self-Control -

CONTROLLING AGGRESSION

Purpose: Help students learn strategies for using assertive behavior as a way to maintain self-control.

Tell the students:

> It is important that we are aware of the difference between assertive and aggressive behaviors and the impact those behaviors have on self-control. This activity helps us learn more about that impact. Please listen, follow directions, and participate.

Have a discussion about assertive and aggressive behaviors and define the differences with the students.

Divide the students into groups. Ask each group to brainstorm ways they can control themselves and use assertive behavior instead of aggressive behavior.

Ask each small group to role-play one of their assertive behavior strategies for the larger group.

Point out the benefits of assertive behavior. Ask students to discuss the differences and the impact of both behavior choices on their self-control.

Materials:

None

 © 2003
www.allsucceed.com

GROUP COOPERATION

Group Cooperation:

The perception of how one relates to working in a group in reference to the group's members.

The ability to be responsible and dependable when completing group projects.

The ability to demonstrate a commitment and attitude of quality and to give one's best effort in and for the group.

- Group Cooperation -

CONFORMITY EXPERIENCE

Purpose: Help students learn strategies for working effectively in groups when completing group projects.

Tell the students:

> It is important that we learn ways to work effectively in groups when completing group projects. Everyone in a group counts on each other. This activity will give us practice. Please listen, follow directions, and participate.

To focus on the conformity and nonconformity of individuals in groups, ask the group to participate in this role-play guessing game.

Groups of four students could each convey an action to the rest of the class through role-play. Students in each group can draw lots to determine their roles. For example, one student might be the leader, two students the conformists, and the last student the nonconformist.

The leader could first act out the given action in any way he or she chooses. The two conformists might then take turns mimicking the leader's every movement. The nonconformist could then convey the same action in a way very different from that of the leader. After this, the class can guess the subject of the role-play.

As a follow-up, the class could be asked to cite real examples of conformity and nonconformity in the groups to which they belong. Some sample role-play subjects could include the following:

> Trying to stay awake while watching a TV late movie
>
> Walking into the dentist's office
>
> Hiding the mistake of wearing unmatched shoes to school

Notes:

Materials:

None

Notes:

- Group Cooperation -

YOUR FAMILY MAP

Purpose: Help students learn about group members and their unique contributions to the group.

Tell the students:

> Knowing more about the members of the group helps us learn strategies for working together well. This activity will give us practice. Please listen, follow directions, and participate.

Individuals in a family have similar and different interests.

Give students a local road map or ask them to draw one. Ask each student to develop a code for understanding the information on the map. For example, a dark crayon might be used to follow a main road.

In the lower right-hand corner, ask students to draw or glue figures representing the members of their family, then copy or paste drawings of each member in one or more places of interest along the route. For example, the baby might be put by a zoo, brother by a park, and sister by a museum.

The positions show an interest of each family member. They could be displayed as a general student or group travel guide.

Ask each student to use the map to take another student on a sight-seeing trip that incorporates the interests of the family.

Ask students to explain ways that knowing family member interests is important for group cooperation at home.

Explore ways family interests may be incorporated in school, classroom interests or fun special days, or for career awareness.

Materials:
Map copies or maps found on the Internet
Drawing paper
Drawing supplies

© 2003
www.allsucceed.com

- Group Cooperation -

WHERE ARE YOU?

Purpose: Help students learn strategies for working effectively in groups when completing group projects.

Tell the students:

> It is important to learn ways to work effectively in groups when completing group projects. Everyone in a group counts on each other. This activity will give us practice. Please listen, follow directions, and participate.

Place a line on the board with a character named Marie at one end and a character named George at the other end. Read to the class the description below and have students place their names on the board according to which of the two personalities they tend to be like when they work in a group.

> Marie: She wants to be a part of the group—a very important part. She wants her ideas to be chosen. She starts talking as soon as an idea pops into her head, even if someone else is already talking. If no one seems to be listening, she gets mad and shuts up because her feelings are hurt. She wants to get out of the group when they aren't doing things her way.

> George: When he works in a group, he likes to hear their ideas. He listens when others talk and works to understand the meaning behind the words they say. He thinks about what is happening in the group and gives ideas and opinions when he thinks he has an idea to share. He wants to give his best.

Ask students to discuss ideas that can help Marie and George get along better and work more cooperatively in a group. Ask students who have signed up under Marie and those who have signed up under George to form teams to help each other with cooperative group behaviors.

Notes:

Materials:
None

Notes:

- Group Cooperation -

GROUP WORK EXPERIENCE

Purpose: Help students learn strategies for working effectively in groups when completing group projects.

Tell the students:

> It is important to learn ways to work effectively in groups when completing group projects. Everyone in a group counts on each other. This activity will give us practice. Please listen, follow directions, and participate.

Give the students an opportunity to experience group work by dividing into groups for free activity time.

Let each group decide what it will work on.

Whatever work they elect to do, it is to be a group project. Help them when necessary by suggesting things they might do together.

Observe the accomplishments of each group and emphasize that it was achieved by working together.

Discuss each group's and group member's experiences.

Ask students to discuss the ways their groups cooperated.

Ask student to determine other times they can use the activity ideas in other life situations.

Materials:

None

Notes:

- Group Cooperation -

HOW DO YOU WORK?

Purpose: Help students learn to demonstrate a commitment, an attitude of quality, and to give their best effort in and for the group.

Tell the students:

It is important to develop an attitude of quality when completing group projects. Giving your best effort and having a commitment to the group are key for that to happen. This activity will give us practice. Please listen, follow directions, and participate.

Discuss with the students how there are three types of workers in a group: the shirker, who gets by with little or no work; the worker, who does his or her job; and the star, who wants to do everything. Discuss, duplicate, or list on the board the following situations:

1. A group of students were going to paint a mural. Each student volunteered to paint a particular part.

2. The students were going to watch a newscast of the latest space launching and report on it. Each student was asked to listen for different things.

3. Three students are building a treehouse together. What could each student do?

4. Three students are supposed to plan an act for a variety show.

Have the students show how each character would probably behave in the situation portrayed. Help the actors reflect upon their own behaviors to determine whether they are a shirker, worker, or star.

Discuss with the group how it feels to be a shirker, worker, or star, and how it feels working together with such persons.

Materials:

None

Notes:

- Group Cooperation -

CREATING NEW COUNTRIES

Purpose: Help students learn strategies for demonstrating leadership and working effectively in groups to complete a group project.

Tell the students:

> It is important to learn ways to work and be an effective leader in groups. Everyone in a group counts on each other. This activity will give us practice. Please listen, follow directions, and participate.

This activity may be as simple or as extensive as you wish. It is important that it be handled in an inductive manner, allowing leadership to emerge. This activity can be incorporated easily into a social studies project.

Begin by having the students divide into at least two groups, with each group pretending to be a new country. Define boundaries on the classroom floor. Rules, authority, government, and all regulations could evolve and change as students discuss and experience various ideas.

Sophistication, length, and style of this activity depend on the interest and the type of classroom structure. The activities could be a way of conducting your class for an indefinite time in the open classroom or for a designated period of time in the more traditional classroom.

Materials:

None

© 2003
www.allsucceed.com

- Group Cooperation -

GET THE WHOLE PICTURE

Purpose: Help students learn strategies for working effectively in groups when completing group projects.

Before this activity, partially complete a picture jigsaw puzzle.

Tell the students:

> It is important to learn ways to work effectively in groups when completing group projects. Everyone in a group counts on each other. This activity will give us practice. Please listen, follow directions, and participate.

Do not show the students what the completed puzzle will look like.

Divide the students into groups. Ask them to decide on the theme and other information about the puzzle based on the completed puzzle position.

Ask the students to think about the incomplete area. What do the visible clues lead them to believe is in the missing section? Each group could have a spokesperson tell what conclusions they have reached.

Ask the students to explain how they decided what was missing in the puzzle and the reasons they were or were not successful.

Notes:

Materials:

Jigsaw puzzle

Notes:

- Group Cooperation -

EVERYONE BENEFITS

Purpose: Help students learn strategies for making group decisions.

Tell the students:

> Knowing more about the way to make group decisions is important. Those decisions need to consider everyone in the group. This activity will give us practice. Please listen, follow directions, and participate.

Read the following story to the class; then have volunteers tell how they would spend the $1,000 or write a composition and share it with the class.

> "I have good news," father announced at dinner. " We will be getting a refund of over $1,000 on last year's income tax. At first I thought I'd buy some new equipment for my job. But I could get along without it for awhile longer. I thought maybe you would have some ideas about how to spend it."
>
> "How about spending it on a new lawn mower, Dad?" asked Bill hopefully. "It sure would be easier to mow the grass, or maybe we could get a new TV or a minibike! Those would be fun!"
>
> "But, how about a dishwasher? Then we wouldn't have to wash dishes."
>
> "How about a vacation? We would all enjoy getting away for a few days and this money could help us do it."
>
> "Wow! A trip to Disneyland!" laughed Bill.
>
> Father laughed, "Let's not make any snap decisions before we spend the money. Let's think of ways the money can benefit the whole family."

Materials:
None

Ask students to brainstorm ideas that can benefit the whole family. Relate the ideas to possible projects that can benefit all students in the class or that can be used for service learning possibilities.

www.allsucceed.com

- Group Cooperation -

THINGS DONE WELL

Purpose: Help students learn about group members and their unique contributions to the group.

Tell the students:

> Knowing more about the members of the group helps us learn strategies for working together well. This activity will give us practice. Please listen, follow directions, and participate.

The students in a classroom were talking about families. Jack showed a picture of his mother. "She likes to read to my brother, Tom," he told the class. "My father likes numbers, and he can do them better than I can."

Lisa held up a picture of her twin brother. "He likes sports," she said, "but he doesn't like schoolwork as well as I do."

Everyone learns in a different way.

Discuss:
    Can anyone do well (or be best) at everything?
    Explain the reasons some people do one thing well and other things poorly.
    Name the different things that members of your family can do well.

Ask each student to make a list of things he or she can do well. Discuss and compare lists.

Discuss how the lists of strengths can be used to support group cooperation at school and at home.

Notes:

Materials:

None

Notes:

- Group Cooperation -

SHARING TRADITIONS

Purpose: Help students learn about group members and their unique contributions to the group.

Tell the students:

> Knowing more about the members of the group helps us learn strategies for working together well. This activity will give us practice. Please listen, follow directions, and participate.

Each family has its own traditional way of preparing for or celebrating a holiday.

Using topless shoe boxes, ask students to cut away one side to make a stage. Dolls, cutouts, or drawings could be set in the box to show students' families' typical observance of a special day.

Students might find out from parents, relatives, and friends how these traditions originated. A display could be set up in the room.

Students with similar traditions can form a group and choose a person to act as a representative to tell about the customs.

The boxes can be rearranged by countries, holidays, activities, and people involved to show similarities and differences in traditions.

Materials:
Shoe boxes
 or other small
 boxes
Drawing paper
Drawing supplies
Art supplies

© 2003
www.allsucceed.com

- Group Cooperation -

BECOMING INDEPENDENT

Purpose: Help students learn strategies to be independent as appropriate to support the group.

Tell the students:

> It is important to learn to be independent and do things we are able to do. Everyone in a group counts on each other. This activity will give us practice. Please listen, follow directions, and participate.

Lead a discussion related to overprotection and overdependence. Have the students list at least three activities he or she can do at home to let his or her parents know how independent he or she can be—if given the opportunity.

Ask students to determine the effect on

1. relationships at home

2. relationships at school

when students do activities they are capable and permitted to do.

Relate the ideas generated to ways of supporting group cooperation.

Notes:

Materials:

None

© 2003
www.allsucceed.com

Notes:

- Group Cooperation -

EVERY-DAY ROUTINES

Purpose: Help students learn about group members, their routines, and their impact on the group.

Tell the students:

> Knowing more about the members of the group and their routines helps us learn strategies for working together well. This activity will give us practice. Please listen, follow directions, and participate.

A family sets up certain routines to keep the day running smoothly and each member has his or her own routine that he or she works into the family schedule.

Ask the students to write down their own routines and those of other members of their family. Since routines tend to be taken for granted, suggest different phases of routines, including

- responsibilities
- interests
- fun
- what is done throughout the day (e.g., in the morning, after dinner, and before bedtime.)

Some other things that can be noted are differences in routines among family members. How are they different? Explain the reasons they differ.

Some funny or unusual things about family routines could be listed. Information about pets and their routines could also be collected.

Materials:

Optional:
 Drawing paper
 Drawing supplies

With all this data about family routines, the students might like to make up a song or poem about their families. The melody for a song could be taken from a camp song, preferably one with a chorus repeated after each stanza. The chorus could be about the family as a group, and each stanza could be about a different family member.

Discuss the way routines at home support family harmony. Explore ways that routines at school support harmony and learning.

© 2003
www.allsucceed.com

- Group Cooperation -

POSITIVE HOME ENVIRONMENT

Purpose: Help students learn strategies to improve behavior and interaction between group members.

Tell the students:

> Knowing more about ways to behave and interact helps us learn strategies for working together well. This activity will give us practice. Please listen, follow directions, and participate.

Discuss with the group that family environment has an effect on personality development. Respect for the feelings of others is an important part of family living.

Discuss topics such as:
1. sharing
2. helping others
3. controlling anger

Ask students the way those behaviors affect a person's personality.

Ask the students the effect those behaviors have on cooperation.

Relate the activity ideas to ways of improving the classroom environment.

Optional: Have the students view a TV program related to family life and discuss how TV families do and do not represent the typical family.

Notes:

Materials:

None

Notes:

- Group Cooperation -

LEARNING FROM ANIMALS

Purpose: Help students learn about animal behavior and the similarities and differences from groups of people.

Tell the students:

> Knowing more about animal behavior helps us learn ways we are different and similar with groups. This activity will give us practice. Please listen, follow directions, and participate.

If there are pets in the classroom or learning center such as fish, hamsters, mice, or an ant farm, each student might have a turn caring for and observing the animals. Ask students to start a booklet explaining each kind of animal.

On blank pages at the back of the book, ask students to take turns making notes on animal behavior. After everyone has had a turn, small groups could use this record of information to report to the class activities of animal families.

Ask students to determine the following:

1. How are animal families similar to and different from human families?
2. Do they show affection?
3. Care for each other?
4. Have different responsibilities?
5. How is each animal different from others in its family?

Ask students to discuss their answers.

Relate the activity ideas to cooperation in the classroom as appropriate.

Materials:
Classroom or school pets/ animals
Notebook
Resource information

© 2003
www.allsucceed.com

Notes:

- Group Cooperation -

JEALOUSY AWARENESS

Purpose: Help students learn strategies to improve feeling communication between group members.

Tell the students:

> Knowing more about ways to communicate about our feelings helps us learn strategies for working together well. This activity will give us practice. Please listen, follow directions, and participate.

Discuss with the class group the normalcy of jealous feelings and how it is possible to dissipate them by speaking of them with others.

Have the students role-play for the class one situation in which a family's jealousies are resolved by talking over the problem together. Examples are:

1. a new baby in the family

2. a parent appearing to favor one child

Ask students to add other situations when they felt jealousy.

Ask students to determine the best person to speak with about each situation presented. This could help them to express the feeling and better understand each situation.

Relate ways the ideas could improve relationships at school.

Materials:

None

Notes:

- Group Cooperation -

IMPROVING RELATIONSHIPS

Purpose: Help students learn strategies for handling conflict in the group.

Tell the students:

> Knowing more about the way to handle group conflict is important. The results of conflict affects everyone in the group. This activity will give us practice. Please listen, follow directions, and participate.

Discuss with the group how most families have conflicts between parents and children.

Ask the students what causes the majority of conflicts between them and their parents and list the following conflict areas on the board:

> home duties
>
> friends
>
> money
>
> social life
>
> time spent on homework
>
> clothes or personal appearance

Discuss the fact that these conflicts arise because of a student's desire for self-reliance and independence. Ask students to suggest ways to resolve these conflicts.

Ask students to determine ways the conflict areas can cause conflicts at school.

Ask students to develop a plan to improve relationships at home and at school based on this information.

Materials:
None

- Group Cooperation -

CONSIDERING FAMILY MEMBERS

Purpose: Help students learn strategies for demonstrating helpful behavior that improves group relationships.

Tell the students:

> Knowing more about the way our behavior helps a group is important. Those behavior decisions affect everyone in the group. This activity will give us practice. Please listen, follow directions, and participate.

Have a class discussion about relationships within the family.

Divide the class into groups of four to six to discuss situations illustrating that brothers and sisters are important family members.

Give examples of sharing, consideration, and fairness to brothers and sisters.

Have the class list specific ways one can be considerate toward family members.

Ask the group to select items on the list to role-play.

If students have no siblings, ask them to determine the effects of having no siblings at home and at school.

Notes:

Materials:

None

Notes:

- Group Cooperation -

STRENGTH IN NUMBERS

Purpose: Help students learn to be responsible and dependable when completing group projects.

Tell the students:

It is important to learn to be dependable and responsible when completing group projects. Everyone in a group counts on each other. This activity will give us practice. Please listen, follow directions, and participate.

Discuss with the class the value of cooperation in carrying out group plans.

Give each student a small twig, about 18 inches long, and dry and thin enough to be broken easily. Have each student try to break the stick, which he or she probably will be able to do. Then gather the sticks into a bundle and ask if anyone can break them now that they are in a bundle.

Following the object lesson, read Aesop's Fable, "The Bundle of Sticks."

Identify with the group some goals they value in common, such as participation in music or enjoyment of team sports.

Also discuss the reasons these goals cannot be achieved unless everyone cooperates.

Ask students to apply the concepts to situations at school and at home.

Materials:
18" small twigs
Aesop's Fable, "Bundle of Sticks"

© 2003
www.allsucceed.com

256

Notes:

- Group Cooperation -

GROUP IDENTITY

Purpose: Help students understand different kinds of groups and learn to be responsible and dependable when completing group projects.

Tell the students:

> It is important to learn about different kinds of groups and to be dependable and responsible when completing group projects. Everyone in a group counts on each other. This activity will give us practice. Please listen, follow directions, and participate.

Discuss with the students how they often can be a member of a group without even realizing it, and sometimes they may overlook how important these groups can be. Give a recent example appropriate for your group, such as a reading group, a clean-up committee, or a committee planning a party.

Ask the following questions:

1. Did those of you who were working together on that project realize you were a part of a group?

2. Can you think of some other projects you have worked on as a member of a group in our class?

Compile a list on the board under the heading, Classroom Groups. Then ask, "Can you think of some other groups that you are a member of or have been a member of in this school?" (e.g., safety patrol, student council, etc.)

Compile a list on the board under the heading, Small Groups. Then ask, "Can you think of some groups you belong to outside of the classroom and school?" (e.g., living unit, church, club, etc.)

Compile a list on the board under the heading, Community Groups. Ask students to list groups to which they belong.

Ask students to identify their feelings while being a part of the group and ways they contributed and learned. Relate the information to possible service learning projects.

Materials:

None

Notes:

- Group Cooperation -

MOSAIC EXPERIENCE

Purpose: Help students learn strategies for working effectively in groups when completing group projects.

Tell the students:

> It is important to learn ways to work effectively in groups when completing group projects. Everyone in a group counts on each other. This activity will give us practice. Please listen, follow directions, and participate.

Divide the students into three groups and give each group 12 green color chips and 12 yellow color chips. Ask each group to arrange a mosaic using exactly 24 chips. Encourage the students as they work together as a group.

Then ask each group to arrange a mosaic using 36 chips. Since each group has only 24 chips, one group will not be able to accomplish this task alone. When the students become aware of this difficulty, ask, "Since you don't have enough chips to arrange this mosaic, what can you do?" Lead students to see that one group could split and join the other two groups, bringing 12 chips to each group so that two groups could complete the task.

To conclude the activity, ask:

1. When you can't get something done because you don't have enough materials to work with, what can you do?

2. When there is a specific task to be done, does it matter how it gets done?

3. Does working together in a group get things done faster or better? Please explain.

4. Explain individual responsibilities required of each group member for an effective group.

Materials:
36 green chips
36 yellow chips

- Group Cooperation -

AN EFFECTIVE FOLLOWER

Notes:

Purpose: Help students learn their perception of how they relate to working in a group in reference to group members.

Tell the students:

> You are an important member and needed for your group to work well. Understanding the way we see ourselves and the way we relate to others when we work in a group helps us learn ways to improve. This activity will give us practice. Please listen, follow directions, and participate.

Divide the students into four group and have each group choose two recorders. Tell the group to think of all the characteristics to describe an effective follower.

After 10 minutes, have the recorders report the ideas their group has suggested. On the board, make a master list of the group's suggestions, including each idea only once.

Then ask the students in each group to select the three characteristics from the master list that they consider to be most important in a follower. Ask them to give reasons for each choice.

Discuss the following questions:

1. How can it help you to know the most important characteristics of an effective follower?
2. What can you do to become an effective follower?

Ask students to suggest the names of several persons who are effective followers and to explain the reason they think so.

Materials:

None

Ask students to explain the reason that effective followers can be effective leaders at other times.

Relate the activity ideas to life situations at school and at home.

© 2003
www.allsucceed.com

Notes:

- Group Cooperation -

SHARING A LIST

Purpose: Help students learn about group members and their unique contributions to the group.

Tell the students:

> Knowing more about the interests of members of the group helps us learn strategies for working together well. This activity will give us practice. Please listen, follow directions, and participate.

Ask the students to make a list or draw a picture of things that are fun to share.

Ask students to share their list or picture with the group.

Make a list of student comments on the board.

Ask students to identify others in the group that enjoy sharing similar things.

Ask students to discuss ways this fun information could support cooperation and learning in the class.

Ask students to share fun things with the group as appropriate.

Materials:
Optional:
 Drawing paper
 Drawing supplies

© 2003
www.allsucceed.com

Notes:

- Group Cooperation -

CREATING FAMILY HARMONY

Purpose: Help students learn strategies for improving family group relationships.

Tell the students:

> You are an important member and needed for your family group to work well. Understanding the way we see ourselves and the way we relate to others when we work in a group helps us learn ways to improve. This activity will give us practice. Please listen, follow directions, and participate.

Discuss with the students how privileges that parents may give older brothers and sisters may cause jealousy and anger among younger siblings, often causing quarrels which disrupt family harmony.

Discuss solutions to family quarreling and ask for ideas from the students.

Examples:

> The older child may share a favorite book, toy or possession (with supervision, of course) with the younger child.
>
> The older child may share time playing favorite games with the younger child.
>
> The older child may promise to take the younger child to some special place or activity that the younger child would not be able to go to alone.

Discuss ways these activities may improve relationships and support greater cooperation.

Ask students to relate these ideas to group cooperation in other places.

Explore possible applications for service learning projects.

Materials:

None

Notes:

- Group Cooperation -

FOLLOW MY LEAD

Purpose: Help students learn strategies for giving and following directions.

Duplicate and distribute the Follow My Lead activity sheet.

Form groups of four to six students each. Have each group elect a leader. Give each student a pencil and three copies of the activity sheet. Ask each leader to draw a geometric design on one of the activity sheets without permitting other students to see the drawing. Then have the leader instruct the group on how to draw the design. Example: Place your pencil where line 6 across and line C down meet. Draw a line from this point to line D down and line 4 across. Then draw a line on line D down and stop on line 8 across, etc. Demonstrate this for students. After the leader has told them how to draw the design, compare the students' designs with the leaders.

Discuss the following questions with the students:

1. How did you feel when you were following directions?

2. How did you feel when you were giving instructions?

```
    A   B   C   D   E   F   G   H
1
2
3
4
5
6
7
8
9
```

Materials:

Activity sheet

Discuss ways of applying activity concepts to learning and other life situations.

- **Activity sheet** -

Follow My Lead

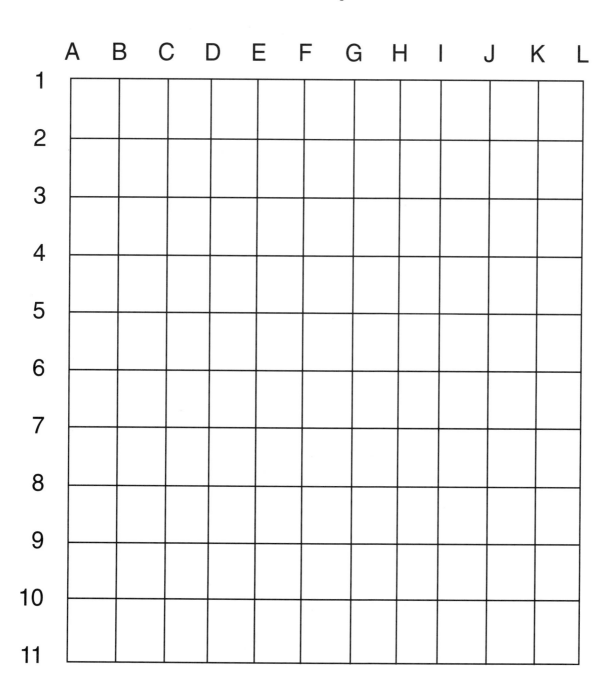

263

Notes:

- Group Cooperation -

COOPERATION EXPERIENCES

Purpose: Help students learn to demonstrate a commitment, an attitude of quality, and to give their best effort in and for the group.

Tell the students:

> It is important to develop an attitude of quality when completing group projects. Giving your best effort and having a commitment to the group are key for that to happen. This activity will give us practice. Please listen, follow directions, and participate.

Ask students to participate in the following cooperation activities and report their results.

1. Have the students perform a stunt that involves working together cooperatively. Have two students hold the ends of a board and balance a ball resting on the board. Have them walk from one side of the room to the other, keeping the ball in balance. If the students work together cooperatively, the ball will remain balanced, and they will complete the activity without a mishap.

2. Now the students are ready to examine the idea of working together cooperatively. Choose 8 to 10 of your less vigorous students and have them role-play a fire drill in which everyone pushes and rushes to get through the door first. After the role-playing, discuss what might happen to those who fell and to those who could not get through the door.

3. Allow 8 or 10 other students to role-play the correct way to conduct a fire drill. Discuss with the students how working together cooperatively is desirable.

Ask students to discuss feelings while observing and participating in each experience. Relate the activity ideas to life situation applications.

Materials:
Ball
Board

Notes:

- Group Cooperation -

CAREER COOPERATION

Purpose: Help students learn about behaviors needed for cooperation in different careers and at school.

Tell the students:

> Knowing more about behaviors needed for cooperation helps us learn strategies for working together well. This activity will give us practice. Please listen, follow directions, and participate.

Help the students see how many occupations depend on people working together.

Ask students to draw pictures of one person who helps in a group (e.g., football player, police officer, plane or train crew member, construction worker, etc.)

Ask students to share their drawings with the group. Ask them to include the role cooperation plays in the person's ability to do the job illustrated.

Ask students to determine ways cooperation helps students do their job at school, just like the people in the drawings.

Ask students to list the behaviors needed to cooperate in their drawing situations and in school.

Materials:

Drawing paper
Drawing supplies

Notes:

- Group Cooperation -

CLASSROOM IMPROVEMENT

Purpose: Help students learn strategies for making group decisions.

Tell the students:

> Knowing more about the way to make group decisions is important. Those decisions need to consider everyone in the group. This activity will give us practice. Please listen, follow directions, and participate.

Divide the students into small groups to talk about situations within the classroom that may be improved.

Before beginning, review guidelines and ground rules for small groups. Ask students to consider the following small group suggestions:

1. During the first few experiences with group work, choose students whom you think may work well together to form a group.

2. Form small groups at first (2 to 3 students each).

3. Pick a group leader whom you think may be able to call on others, keep things going, and report back to the class.

4. Move from group to group to support and assist when necessary.

Between group sessions, ask students to observe and consider possible ways of making improvements.

Then in the next session, ask the students to come together as a class and share ideas for improvement.

Ask students to determine the effectiveness of the groups based on cooperation and following group rules and guidelines.

Relate the ideas generated from the group to other life situations.

Materials:
None

Notes:

- Group Cooperation -

IMPROVING COMMUNICATION

Purpose: Help students learn strategies to improve communication between group members.

Tell the students:

> Knowing more about ways to communicate helps us learn strategies for working together well. This activity will give us practice. Please listen, follow directions, and participate.

Discuss with the students reasons for failure in communication between parents and children. Ask them to discuss what they can do to avoid such situations.

Let the students prepare a role-play portraying the absence or presence of communication between the child and parents.

Discuss the role-play. Ask each member of the audience to brainstorm the following:

1. Three ways to improve communication challenges outlined in the play if the role-play demonstrated challenges.

2. Three reasons the communication was effective if the role-play demonstrated cooperation.

Ask students to determine other times they can use this information.

Materials:

None

Notes:

- Group Cooperation -

IMPROVING COOPERATION

Purpose: Help students learn strategies to improve cooperation and sharing between group members.

Tell the students:

> Knowing more about ways to share and cooperate helps us learn strategies for working together well. This activity will give us practice. Please listen, follow directions, and participate.

Discuss with the students the importance of cooperation and sharing.

Ask the students to role-play and discuss these two situations:

1. "It isn't fair," sharing problems with friends.

2. "What program to watch," conflict over TV program.

Role-play examples of sharing and cooperating in other activities generated by the group.

Ask students to determine ideas to improve their cooperating and sharing with others.

Ask students to determine one thing that they are willing to do as a group and individually. Ask the students to report back their results.

Materials:

None

© 2003
www.allsucceed.com

- Group Cooperation -

USING OUR SENSES

Purpose: Help students learn strategies for using their senses in solving group problems.

Tell the students:

> It is important to learn ways our senses (e.g., smell, touch, sight, sound, and taste) help us solve group problems. This activity will give us practice. Please listen, follow directions, and participate.

Divide the students into groups. Give each group a bag with something inside and close the bag securely.

Let students feel, smell, and shake the bag to see what they can discover about the object through various senses. See if they can guess what it is.

Ask the student groups to discuss the experience. Ask them to discover ways they determined what was in the bag. Ask them to list the senses they used and what they learned by observing other group members who were working to solve the mystery.

Ask each small group to share things they learned with the large group. Make a list of ideas on the board.

Ask students to determine ways the senses can help in working together in other groups and situations.

Notes:

Materials:

Bags
Objects to put
in the bag

Notes:

- Group Cooperation -

WHO SAID IT?

Purpose: Help students learn strategies for being tactful and considerate of others in a group, and the impact of that behavior on feelings between group members.

Tell the students:

> Knowing more about ways to communicate helps us learn strategies for working together well. This activity will give us practice. Please listen, follow directions, and participate.

Discuss with students how a group depends on tact and consideration of other people's feelings. Write the following names on the board, explaining that they are fictitious group members:

Tommie Tattle	Bossy Barbara
Sharon Share	Helpful Harvey
Wanda Worker	Discussion Derric
Marcus My Way	Fedrico First

Then read the following comments, explaining that they were overheard while these eight people were planning a school play. Have the students guess which group member made each statement.

> I have it all figured out.
> Listen to me!
> You stop that or I'll tell.
> I'm going to be the announcer.
> I can do that if it needs to be done.
> We could take turns pulling the curtain.
> If you need help with the backdrop, I can give you a hand.
> I don't want to do it that way! Let's talk it over and then decide.

Follow with discussion, allowing students to give reasons for their choices.

Materials:
None

© 2003
www.allsucceed.com

- **Group Cooperation** -

GOING ON THE AIR

Notes:

Purpose: Help students learn strategies for working effectively in groups when completing group projects.

Tell the students:

> It is important to learn ways to work effectively in groups when completing group projects. Everyone in a group counts on each other. This activity will give us practice. Please listen, follow directions, and participate.

Groups can often accomplish what individuals alone could never do. One of the many reasons for this is that groups can pool the special talents of their members and thus develop more effective programs of action.

Demonstrate this by asking the group to work in small groups on a project that would be too demanding or too burdensome for individual effort.

For example, the group can be divided into three smaller groups to plan and produce their culminating activity for the year, or the group can be divided into three smaller groups to plan and produce a difficult assignment built on easier lessons completed as individual assignments.

First, introduce this idea as if each student would be expected to single-handedly write, direct, get props for, find costumes for, and act out his or her own television show. Students might then be asked to react to this idea. The students might then suggest the need for groups to accomplish some things successfully.

Arrange students in groups according to the distribution of their talents. Each production group might need a director, two or three writers, a props specialist, a costumer, and actors and actresses.

Materials:

None

Ask students to explore other projects that may be best done in a small group. Determine the possibility of using one of their ideas for service learning projects for the group.

© 2003
www.allsucceed.com

Notes:

- Group Cooperation -

GROUP CLEAN-UP DAY

Purpose: Help students learn strategies for working effectively in groups when completing group projects.

Tell the students:

> It is important to learn ways to work effectively in groups when completing group projects. Everyone in a group counts on each other. This activity will give us practice. Please listen, follow directions, and participate.

Discuss the organization of a clean-up day.

On the playground, for example, organize the following:

1. areas to be taken care of
2. equipment to be used
3. students for each area
4. criteria for a good performance on the job

Organize a clean-up on the playground and appoint or let volunteers participate in the group of their choice. Following the clean-up, discuss the feelings of satisfaction experienced.

Ask the students to determine things they did that either helped the efforts or hurt the efforts for success.

Materials:
None

Relate ideas generated from the activity to other life situations.

© 2003
www.allsucceed.com

- Group Cooperation -

SHARING MIRROR

Purpose: Help students learn strategies to improve sharing between group members.

Tell the students:

> Knowing more about ways to share helps us learn strategies for working together well. This activity will give us practice. Please listen, follow directions, and participate.

Ask the students to look into a sharing mirror and tell about someone who has helped them by sharing.

After everyone has shared their information, ask the students to state their feelings when students shared with them and when they shared with others.

The appropriate Feeling Words Cards and Feeling Words Lists activity sheets found beginning on page 293 may be helpful in identifying feeling possibilities.

Ask students to discuss times they might have felt better and enjoyed working in groups better when they shared.

Notes:

Materials:

Optional:
 Mirror
 Feeling Words
  Lists and Cards

Notes:

- Group Cooperation -

BALANCE EXPERIENCES

Purpose: Help students learn strategies for having balance in areas of their life.

Tell the students:

> Knowing more about ways to have balance in areas of our life is important. This activity will help us explore ideas. Please listen, follow directions, and participate.

Balance can be achieved by working together cooperatively. Most students will be familiar with some kind of balance (e.g., teeter-totter, number balances, or the balances in grocery stores, a level for hanging pictures, etc.).

Show a balance, or one of the other examples, to the group so they will have a concrete understanding of what balance is and the way it works. Have the students look at the balance and describe its function.

Allow the students to use the balance while you explain how it works. They will probably say that a balance is used to equalize two things. Make sure all students can see the balance when it is balanced and when it is unbalanced. Also, emphasize that you need to look at both sides.

After using a balance, the students could balance themselves. If you do not have a balance beam, the students could walk, balancing books on their heads, or do some exercises in which balance is essential.

Discuss with the students the idea that people need balance in areas of their life. Ask students to list ways that working in cooperative groups supports having life balance.

Materials:
A small level or items that show balance

Include a discussion of feelings they have when the areas of their lives are in balance. The Feeling Words Cards and Feeling Words Lists Activity Sheets may help them identify feelings in balance situations.

 © 2003
www.allsucceed.com

- Group Cooperation -

EFFECTIVE LEADERSHIP

Purpose: Help students learn strategies for demonstrating leadership and working effectively in groups.

Tell the students:

It is important to learn ways to work and be an effective leader in groups. Everyone in a group counts on each other. This activity will give us practice. Please listen, follow directions, and participate.

Divide the group into four groups and have each group choose two recorders. Tell the groups to think of all the characteristics of an effective leader.

After 10 minutes, have the recorders report the ideas their groups have suggested. Make a master list on the board, including each idea only once.

Then ask each group to select the three characteristics from the master list they consider to be most important in a leader. Have them give their reasons for each choice.

Discuss the following questions:

1. How can it help you to know the most important characteristics of an effective leader?

2. What can you do to become an effective leader?

Ask students to suggest the names of several persons who are effective leaders. Give them time to explain their choices.

Ask students to determine other applications of the ideas generated from this activity.

Notes:

Materials:
None

Notes:

- Group Cooperation -

GROUP PROBLEM SOLVING

Purpose: Help students learn strategies for making group decisions.

Tell the students:

> Knowing more about the way to make group decisions is important. Those decisions need to consider everyone in the group. This activity will give us practice. Please listen, follow directions, and participate.

Discuss with the students the fact that, occasionally, the group is better at solving problems than the individual is.

Distribute an unfinished story to the class. Divide the group into smaller groups (3 or 4 students in each) and direct each group to complete the story.

Ask student groups to read the endings to the group.

Have a discussion after each story ending and ask the group the way it created the story ending.

Ask students to include:

1. ending alternatives
2. choices made from alternatives
3. consequences of each alternative
4. reasons for choice

Ask students to determine times they can use the ideas generated from the activity.

Materials:

Unfinished short stories or story starters

- Group Cooperation -

LEARNING COOPERATION

Purpose: Help students learn about group members, their unique contributions to the group, and ways to help others.

Tell the students:

> Knowing more about the members of the group helps us learn strategies for working together and helping others. This activity will give us practice. Please listen, follow directions, and participate.

Have a discussion about belonging to groups and about group cooperation.

Then divide the group into smaller groups of four to six students each. Ask each group member to write the name of one activity in which he or she wishes to improve.

Ask students to share these activities with other members of the group with this purpose in mind: To find a student who excels in a certain activity to help a student who wishes to improve in the identical activity.

Ask the group to discuss how group cooperation has helped them.

Follow with matching students who wish to improve with someone who excels in that area.

Optional: Post these "needs" and "areas of excellence" on a board. Allow students to add to and make their own arrangements for student cooperative support.

Notes:

Materials:

None

Notes:

- Group Cooperation -

SWEET REWARDS

Purpose: Help students learn strategies for working effectively in groups when completing a group project.

Tell the students:

It is important to learn ways to work effectively in groups when completing a group project. Everyone in a group counts on each other. This activity will give us practice. Please listen, follow directions, and participate.

The activity of making candy allows students to see that ordinary activities often involve cooperation. Cooperation is necessary in two ways: obtaining the ingredients and following directions. Ask the students to bring in the ingredients for a recipe. Those students not assigned to bring ingredients may follow directions or clean up. The recipe will make enough for a group of thirty.

Peanut Butter Creams

Need: large mixing bowl
mixing spoon
measuring cups
spatula
cookie sheet
wax paper
1/4 cup of confectioner's sugar
1 cup of chocolate chips
1/2 cup sweetened condensed milk
1 cup peanut butter.

Directions: Put the sugar in the bowl
Add chocolate chips, condensed milk and peanut butter
Stir everything together with the spoon
Drop pieces onto wax paper placed on top of cookie sheet
Chill candy for a short time (1/2 hour)

Eat and enjoy candy. Select a different recipe depending on group dietary needs.

Materials:
Ingredients for candy

© 2003
www.allsucceed.com

Notes:

- Group Cooperation -

PASSWORD GAME

Purpose: Help students learn information about group dynamics and a means of focusing on the importance of group acceptance.

Tell the students:

It is important to learn ways to work effectively in groups when completing group projects. Everyone in a group counts on each other. This activity will give us practice. Please listen, follow directions, and participate.

This game is an exercise in group dynamics and a means of focusing on the importance of group acceptance. The group can be divided into six groups by asking students to draw construction squares, or "membership cards," of six different colors.

Each color group would then do two things:

1. elect a group leader
2. choose a secret password, a one word feeling word

Explain to the students that learning another group's password is the means of acceptance into that group. Ask each of the six group leaders to take a turn at the board and mark out blank spaces for each letter in his group's password. Students from other groups would then attempt to learn the password by guessing individual letters. Correct guesses are recorded in the appropriate blank spaces. Each incorrect guess allows the leader to write one letter of the word password. A student who wants to guess on paper may write his guess and show it to a member of that group for acceptance or rejection. There is no penalty for rejection.

Guessing ends when the leader completes the password. The Feeling Words Lists activity sheets found beginning on page 293 may help generate feeling word ideas.

Discuss the different passwords that groups in school or in other settings may have. Ask students if it is easy or difficult to determine a group's password.

Ask students to relate this experience to life situations and applications.

Materials:

Six different
  colors of paper
Feeling Words
  Lists activity
  sheets

Notes:

- Group Cooperation -

ROPE-JUMPING EXPERIENCE

Purpose: Help students learn strategies to improve cooperation and sharing between group members.

Tell the students:

> Knowing more about ways to share and cooperate helps us learn strategies for working together well. This activity will give us practice. Please listen, follow directions, and participate.

Discuss with the students the importance of cooperation and sharing.

This activity helps the students see that sharing sometime means waiting for someone else to have a turn. This experience may help students develop the ability of have fun in seeing the enjoyment of others.

Divide the class into groups of about five (three students in each group turn the rope and jump, and the other two wait for a turn). Rotate turns so that each student has the opportunity to jump, turn, and wait.

When all have had a turn at all three roles, ask the small groups to return to the larger group.

Ask the students to describe their experience while waiting, jumping, and turning. Ask the group to explain different benefits of all three roles.

Ask students to determine other times to practice this skill.

Optional: Use the same concept using games with older students.

Materials:

Jump rope

- Group Cooperation -

RESPONSIBILITY IN GROUPS

Purpose: Help students learn to be responsible and dependable when completing group projects.

Tell the students:

> It is important to learn to be dependable and responsible when completing group projects. Everyone in a group counts on each other. This activity will give us practice. Please listen, follow directions, and participate.

Discuss with the students the importance of **accepting responsibility and working together as a group**. (These are signs of maturity.)

Ask the students how a first grader would react to situations such as these:

1. playing with a friend and sharing a toy
2. accepting responsibility for helping with work at home or at school
3. being careful when crossing the street

Discuss ways the behavior of an older student would look different.

Ask students to role play behavior that demonstrates responsibility in the situations.

Ask students to compare their conduct with that of an older student.

Allow volunteers to name one specific activity in which they worked with others and ways they benefited.

Notes:

Materials:

None

Notes:

- Group Cooperation -

FAMILY CHALLENGES

Purpose: Help students learn to be responsible, dependable, and respectful when completing family projects and in family relationships.

Tell the students:

> It is important to learn to be dependable, respectful, and responsible with your family members and when doing family jobs. Everyone in a group counts on each other. This activity will give us practice. Please listen, follow directions, and participate.

Families share problems and disagreements as well as joy and happiness.

Divide the students into family groups. Each group could present the following situations on a pretend TV set.

The action is stopped for a "station break" just before the outcome of each presentation. During the break, the members of the audience offer ideas as to how the problem can be solved.

Students could use a problem-solving procedure to assist them. A simple rating sheet could be set up for each student to evaluate each solution—to tell whether the problem was handled in the best manner.

1. Parent is tired of picking up the toys
2. No one likes the supper
3. The children want allowances increased
4. Parent isn't home very often

Materials:

Optional:
  Large appliance box

The class might prefer to propose problems that are important to them.

Optional: Some class members could use a large appliance box to cut out the shape of a TV set.

© 2003
www.allsucceed.com

- Group Cooperation -

SHARING COLLAGE

Purpose: Help students learn strategies to improve cooperation and sharing between group members.

Tell the students:

> Knowing more about ways to share and cooperate helps us learn strategies for working together well. This activity will give us practice. Please listen, follow directions, and participate.

Discuss with the students the importance of cooperation and sharing.

Divide the class into groups of four students each. Tell students that you want each group to make a collage of people sharing and working together. Have them find some pictures in magazines that show people sharing or doing things together. Students cut out the pictures and paste them on construction paper. They may share the materials, share the work to be done, or both.

Give a pair of scissors, glue, and a sheet of construction paper to each group. Place the magazines in a convenient place. Allow students to work out the problems of sharing the material and dividing the work to complete the task.

After the collages have been completed, lead a discussion using these questions:

1. Did you experience any difficulty in sharing the materials?

2. Did you experience any difficulty in sharing the work to be done?

3. In what way is it important to know how to share and cooperate in a group?

Display the collage. Encourage all student efforts.

Notes:

Materials:

Materials for a Collage—
  Paper
  Magazines
  Art supplies

Notes:

- Group Cooperation -

CREATE A MURAL

Purpose: Help students learn to be responsible and dependable when completing group projects.

Tell the students:

> It is important to learn to be dependable and responsible when completing group projects. Everyone in a group counts on each other. This activity will give us practice. Please listen, follow directions, and participate.

Select a story that is appropriate for your group.

Ask the students in the group to design and paint a mural of the story.

Divide into small groups and ask each group to be responsible for a part of the story. Each section is to be attached when finished to make a large mural.

After the groups are finished with their portion of the mural, have a special time to assemble the mural.

Ask students to discuss the behaviors in their group that helped the project.

Materials:
4 large pieces of paper
Paint
Art supplies

© 2003
www.allsucceed.com

Notes:

- Group Cooperation -

RESPONSIBILITIES AND RULES

Purpose: Help students learn strategies for working effectively in groups when completing group projects.

Tell the students:

It is important to learn ways to work effectively in groups when completing group projects. Everyone in a group counts on each other. This activity will give us practice. Please listen, follow directions, and participate.

Discuss with your group the advantage of belonging to a group. Discuss the roles that responsibilities and rules play to make the group a success. Ask students to list rules they think are important to have in their group.

Examples include the following:

1. Members listen when someone speaks.

2. Everyone is willing to do his or her share.

3. Group success results when the members know how to work with others.

Discuss the responsibilities and rules generated from the students.

Ask the students to form small groups and demonstrate what would happen if these rules were and were not followed.

Discuss the feelings of the students after the role-play is complete.

Ask students to determine ways of using the ideas in other situations.

Materials:

None

Notes:

- Group Cooperation -

STUDENT GOVERNMENT

Purpose: Help students learn strategies for making group decisions and solving group-owned problems.

Tell the students:

> Knowing more about the way to make group decisions is important. Those decisions need to consider everyone in the group. This activity will give us practice. Please listen, follow directions, and participate.

Students can organize a Room Council that would meet at least once a week or as often as needed to make rules and to consider problems that arise when these rules are ignored. The sessions would last 15 or 20 minutes. Make certain that all problems are handled in a casual and understanding way.

The following steps may prove helpful in organizing a Room Council:

1. Talk with students about making plans or talking over problems. Ask, "How can we solve our problem? When is the best time?"

2. Decide with the students whether officers are going to be needed and, if so, the duties of each.

3. Set a time for the meetings.

4. Guide students in making a list of qualifications for each office.

Materials:
None

5. Nominations can be given orally in class.

6. Candidates can give campaign talks.

7. Set up a simple procedure or informal discussion group for the meeting.

Students may determine a name for their Room Council.

Notes:

- Group Cooperation -

GROUP PARTICIPATION EXPERIENCE

Purpose: Help students learn strategies for working effectively in groups when completing group projects and assignments.

Tell the students:

> It is important to learn ways to work effectively in groups when completing group projects. Everyone in a group counts on each other. This activity will give us practice. Please listen, follow directions, and participate.

Ask the students to form groups of four to six students. Tell the groups that you want them to prepare a report of the names and eye colors of the members of their group. If there are several people in their group with the same eye color, then find out more specific information about them.

Watch to see if the groups can complete the task. If they are unable to do so or are having trouble, ask:

1. What is slowing your group down?

2. What can you do to prepare the report faster? Would it help to elect a recorder to write down information?

Suggest that each student tell the recorder his or her name and eye color. Some students might not know the color of their eyes and they will have to ask other students. This will lead to looking squarely into each other's faces.

Repeat the activity three or four times to allow all students to participate in several groups.

Ask the students to determine the strategies they used to have successful groups. Ask them to share ways they determined the student to be the recorder. Ask the students to list those things that helped their group and to determine what to do for those things that held the group back.

Materials:

None

Notes:

- Group Cooperation -

MY HOUSE AND FAMILY

Purpose: Help students learn strategies to improve communication between group members.

Tell the students:

> Knowing more about ways to communicate helps us learn strategies for working together well. This activity will give us practice. Please listen, follow directions, and participate.

Give each student a large sheet of paper and crayons. Ask the student to make an outline of his or her house. Then ask students to draw the people in the house.

Using balloons for conversation (similar to a cartoon format), ask students to write what the people are saying.

This activity is designed to lead to a discussion of how and what families communicate. It can also be a jumping-off point for discussing how families live together.

Relate the information to ways that classroom cooperation may be enhanced. Ask students to "test" the ideas and to observe the effects on class cooperation.

Materials:
Large sheets of paper
Drawing supplies

© 2003
www.allsucceed.com

- Group Cooperation -

ASSERTIVE GROUP EFFECTS

Purpose: Help students learn and acknowledge the difference between assertive and aggressive behaviors when they communicate with group members.

Tell the students:

> It is important that we are aware of the difference between assertive and aggressive behaviors and the impact those behaviors have on members of a group. This activity helps us learn more about that impact. Please listen, follow directions, and participate.

Have a discussion about assertive and aggressive behaviors and define the difference with the students:

1. Aggressive behavior is aimed at injuring some person or object, or behavior that would affect another person in a hurtful manner.

2. Assertive behavior is aimed at making positive statements with great confidence, sometimes in the face of opposition.

The students may show their ability to understand assertive behavior by doing a group role-play.

Divide the students into small groups. Ask students to brainstorm examples of times assertive behavior could help groups cooperate better. Then, ask the small groups to role-play one of their ideas for the group.

After the role-plays are complete, ask one member from each group to share the list of other times assertive behavior would help group cooperation.

Point out the benefits of assertive behavior. Ask students to discuss the impact of assertive behavior choices on group members.

Notes:

Materials:

None

FEELING WORDS
LISTS AND CARDS

- Activity Sheet -

Feeling Words

List I

happy	safe	merry
mad	lonely	ashamed
sad	jealous	pleased
glad	alone	beautiful
angry	upset	ugly
worried	loved	unsure
afraid	hurt	outraged
helpful	kind	trusting
hurtful	cruel	trusted
important	sure	fat
proud	excited	skinny

- Activity Sheet -

Feeling Words

List II

obnoxious	sensuous	hysterical
pride	playful	confused
embarrassed	childish	desirable
joyful	fear	interested
anxious	weak	melancholy
cooperative	startled	cold
fascinated	guilty	competitive
sadness	high	astounded
confident	trapped	tired
frustration	furious	freedom
indifferent	selfish	bored

- Activity Sheet -

Feeling Words

List III

uncooperative	suspicious	cheerful
unlucky	disobedient	bright
stupid	friendly	bold
unselfish	impolite	cautious
unpopular	obedient	energetic
creative	popular	honest
courteous	pouty	insecure
dishonest	sassy	lazy
brave	strong	optimistic
pessimistic	lucky	unkind
determined		

Happy	Mad
Sad	Glad
Angry	Worried
Afraid	Helpful
Hurtful	Important

Proud	Safe
Lonely	Jealous
Alone	Upset
Loved	Hurt
Kind	Shy

Obnoxious	Sensuous
Hysterical	Pride
Fear	Cruel
Childish	Startled
Courteous	Strong

Determined	Desirable
Weak	Anxious
Cold	Cooperative
Dishonest	Lazy
Fascinated	Guilty

Competitive	Melancholy
Joy	Interested
Confused	High
Astounded	Confident
Trapped	Tired

Frustration	Furious
Free	Indifferent
Selfish	Bored
Beautiful	Playful
Optimistic	Pessimistic

Embarrassed	Fat
Ashamed	Merry
Pleased	Skinny
Suspicious	Excited
Ugly	Unlucky

Outraged	Unsure
Trusting	Trusted
Sure	Brave
Cheerful	Disobedient
Popular	Honest

Bright	Stupid
Friendly	Bold
Unselfish	Obedient
Energetic	Creative
Sassy	Pouty

Create your own Feeling Words Cards.

- Activity Sheet -

Creative

Corner

Grow with Guidance® Copyright © 2003
www.allsucceed.com

- Activity Sheet -

Creative Corner

Creative Corner

Quality Programs, Materials, and Training That Work!